# HARVARD HISTORICAL MONOGRAPHS
## LX

PUBLISHED UNDER THE DIRECTION
OF THE DEPARTMENT OF HISTORY
FROM THE INCOME OF
THE ROBERT LOUIS STROOCK FUND

# JAMES HOLT

# CONGRESSIONAL INSURGENTS AND THE PARTY SYSTEM 1909-1916

HARVARD UNIVERSITY PRESS
*Cambridge, Massachusetts* 1967

*For My Mother and Father*

# Preface

This study of Republican insurgency began as an investigation into the relationship between the insurgents and the Wilson administration. As a non-American familiar with a political system in which party allegiances are closely related to ideological and social divisions, I had always been fascinated by the more complex role of partisanship in the American political system. The Republican insurgents seemed a classic example of a political faction attached to the "wrong" political party. Clearly they had more in common with the Wilsonian Democrats than with the regular faction of their own party. What then was their attitude to the Wilson administration? Did they ever consider forming a permanent alliance with the Democratic progressives? How did they look upon Theodore Roosevelt's Progressive party? What was their view of their own Republican organization? It was questions such as these that I hoped to answer when I began my research.

I soon found that the insurgents were bitterly hostile to President Wilson and most of his legislative program. At the same time they were cool toward the Progressive party and on bad terms with the Old Guard of the G.O.P. In sum, the insurgents, who in the Taft years had often held the center of the political stage, were by the Wilson years a rather isolated and ineffectual group in national politics. This discovery led me back to the election of 1912 and back again to the great intraparty battles of Taft's administration, so that the scope of the study was considerably enlarged.

Nevertheless I would emphasize that the central concern of this book is still as I originally envisaged it. It is not an attempt at a definitive history of insurgency but a study of the insurgents' role in the party system. I have not attempted to deal with such important questions as the ideology of the insurgents or the origins of the movement except insofar as they bear on the major theme.

# Acknowledgments

Of the many people who helped me to produce this book I wish to thank especially Professor Frank Freidel. His expert supervision of the project in its original form as a doctoral dissertation and his friendly encouragement throughout were greatly appreciated. The manuscript was read at various stages by Barton Bernstein, Arthur Link, and my colleagues at the University of Auckland, Michael Bassett and Robert Chapman. To the last of these I owe much of my original interest in American history. To all of them I offer my thanks for helpful criticism. The University Grants committee of New Zealand provided financial aid to purchase microfilm essential for the completion of the book in New Zealand.

Writing a book is both a rewarding and a burdensome enterprise. My wife Jill shared most of the burdens with me while enjoying few of the rewards.

*Auckland, New Zealand*                                                   James Holt
*July 1967*

# Contents

# Congressional Insurgents
## and the Party System
## 1909-1916

# chapter one

# Introduction

The insurgent Republicans' revolt against the conservative leadership of their party in Congress is one of the most celebrated political movements of the whole "progressive era." Few Democratic or regular Republican Senators are as well remembered as Robert La Follette, George Norris, Albert Beveridge, William Borah, Albert Cummins, or Jonathan Dolliver. Few political battles are more familiar than the assault on the Payne-Aldrich tariff bill in the Senate or the overthrow of Speaker Cannon in the House. The passage of time has done little to dim the insurgents' reputation as outstanding reformers in an age of reform.

Yet in terms of their own specific political goals, the insurgents were largely failures. Certainly the initial impact of their rebellion on American politics was considerable. As individuals, insurgent Republicans scored some significant victories such as La Follette's Seamen's Act and Norris's efforts on behalf of public power. In the states, La Follette, Cummins, and other insurgents led highly effective reform movements. But in national politics, the insurgents as a group became famous mainly for their glorious defeats. They first achieved renown by stubbornly opposing the Payne-Aldrich tariff bill, which passed. They defended the conservation policies of Chief Forester, Gifford Pinchot, who was dismissed. In 1912 they attempted to win the presidency for Theodore Roosevelt, who lost first the Republican nomination and then the election. They fought for a peaceful, noninterventionist foreign policy during the neutrality years from 1914 to 1917, but the United States entered World War I. Above all, they never achieved their main ambition, which was to make the national Republican party an instrument of progressive reform.

The insurgents were most successful when they formed combinations with other parties or factions on some specific issue. Thus in 1910 they joined Democrats to weaken the allegedly dictatorial powers of Speaker Cannon in the House of Representatives and to toughen the Taft administration's railroad legislation. In 1913 they joined radical Democrats to force the adoption of more steeply graduated income taxes, and after the war they helped conservative Republicans defeat the League treaty. But never were they able to consummate these temporary alliances and form a permanent majority coalition. Nor could they achieve anything on their own. Not once did they succeed in electing or even nominating a presidential candidate of whom they wholly approved, and for all their brilliance as legislators, they were never able to match the legislative achievements of the Democrats under Woodrow Wilson. Once during the Taft administration, Senator Dolliver remarked that about the only satisfaction he had derived from his public career had come from the seven years of Theodore Roosevelt's presidency.[1] His lament would serve well as an epitaph for Republican insurgency in general.

The term "insurgent" was used in the Taft and Wilson years to describe political rebels of various kinds, but especially dissident Republicans in Congress. It is difficult to define a group of this type in precise terms, for congressional divisions are notoriously unstable and it is a rare Congressman or Senator who does not break with his party's leaders on one issue or another. Nevertheless the existence of a relatively cohesive insurgent faction within the Republican party in Congress between 1909 and 1916 is indisputable. In these years a group of about ten Republican Senators regularly acted together on a

---

[1] Jonathan P. Dolliver to Gifford Pinchot, March 25, 1910, Theodore Roosevelt Papers, Library of Congress.

a whole range of national issues, meeting constantly to plan strategy in private, openly defying the party's established leaders in public.

In the earlier part of Taft's administration, eight Senators — Beveridge of Indiana, Borah of Idaho, Bristow of Kansas, Clapp of Minnesota, Crawford of South Dakota, Cummins and Dolliver of Iowa, and La Follette of Wisconsin — formed the hard core of this group. Bourne of Oregon, Brown and Burkett of Nebraska, and Dixon of Montana were loosely associated with it. In 1910 Beveridge was defeated and Dolliver died, but Gronna of North Dakota, Kenyon of Iowa, Poindexter of Washington, and Works of California entered the Senate and attached themselves to the insurgent faction in 1911. Norris of Nebraska and Sterling of South Dakota were added in 1913. It is more difficult to ascertain the size of the insurgent group in the House, but it numbered about 40 Representatives during Taft's administration. For example, a caucus of insurgent Congressmen held on April 3, 1911, was attended by 41 Representatives.[2]

The leading insurgents had a great deal in common before the great intraparty battles of the Taft years. Typically the insurgent Senator had migrated as a young man to the state which he later represented in Congress. With the notable exceptions of Albert Beveridge and Robert La Follette, the insurgents left the areas where they had been born, raised, and educated, and rose to political power in states further west. Cummins moved from Pennsylvania to Iowa, Dolliver from West Virginia to Iowa, Poindexter from Tennessee to Washington, Norris from Ohio to Nebraska. Almost to a man, the insurgents were raised on farms, educated at midwestern colleges or universities, and — until they moved to Washington, D.C. — lived all their lives in rural areas, small towns, or small cities.[3]

---

[2] New York *Times,* April 4, 1911.

[3] For background information on the insurgent leaders see the *Biographical Directory of the American Congress, 1774–1949,* House Document 607, 81 Congress, 2 Session. Also, Howard W. Allen, *Miles Poindexter: a Political Biography,* unpublished Ph.D. dissertation,

A small-town legal practice bridged the gap in the insurgents' careers between their early days on farms and in school and their later years in politics. Poindexter practiced law in Walla Walla, and then Spokane, Washington; Crawford in Pierre, South Dakota; Norris in Beaver City and McCook, Nebraska; Dolliver in Dodge City, Iowa; Borah in Boise, Idaho. Bristow, an editor, and Gronna, a merchant with business interests in real estate, insurance, and banking, were the only nonlawyers among the Senate insurgents.

The insurgents did not enter politics as zealous reformers. Political activity was simply a normal supplementary occupation for an ambitious small-town lawyer in the 1880's and 1890's. The insurgents were regular Republicans in their younger days because regular Republicanism was the political creed they had inherited and the dominant political force in the states where they lived. In the mid–1890's, a tide of Populism and Bryanism swept across many of the states that were later represented in Congress by insurgent Republicans, but at this stage men like Cummins, La Follette, and Norris preferred to stick to Republican orthodoxy. Borah, from silver-producing Idaho, was the only important insurgent leader of the Taft years who supported Bryan for the presidency in 1896. Poindexter, a southerner whose father had been a Colonel in the Confederate army, was the one former Democrat

University of Washington, 1959; Calvin Perry Armin, *Coe I. Crawford and the Progressive Movement in South Dakota,* unpublished Ph.D. dissertation, University of Colorado, 1957; Claude G. Bowers, *Beveridge and the Progressive Era* (Cambridge, Mass., 1932); Claudius O. Johnson, *Borah of Idaho* (New York, 1936); Belle and Fola La Follette, *Robert M. La Follette,* 2 vols. (New York, 1953); Richard Lowitt, *George W. Norris: the Making of a Progressive, 1861–1912* (Syracuse, N.Y., 1963); William Weiland Phillips, *The Life of Asle J. Gronna: a Self-made Man of the Prairies,* unpublished Ph.D. dissertation, University of Missouri, 1958; Thomas Richard Ross, *Jonathan Prentiss Dolliver: a Study in Political Integriy and Independence* (Iowa City, 1958); A. Bower Sageser, "Joseph L. Bristow: The Editor's Road to Politics," *Kansas Historical Quarterly,* Summer 1964, p. 153; Ralph Mills Sayre, *Albert Baird Cummins and the Progressive Movement in Iowa,* unpublished Ph.D. dissertation, Columbia University, 1958.

among the Senate insurgents, and he switched to the Republican party during the 1890's because he opposed Bryanite radicalism.

Contrary to that well-known maxim which links radicalism to youth, the insurgents did not emerge as advocates of progressive reform until the first decade of the twentieth century, by which time they were experienced politicians in their forties or fifties. By now a taste for political reform had begun to spread through sections of American society which had earlier been repelled by Bryanism and the threat to property that its inflationary doctrines implied. The insurgents were middle-aged professionals who responded to the new political environment by transforming themselves from McKinley conservatives into progressive reformers.

In many cases, the insurgents made the transition from defender to critic of the status quo during the course of their congressional careers. Men like George Norris, Asle Gronna, Moses Clapp, and Albert Beveridge were first elected to Congress as regular Republicans, but moved gradually to the left during Theodore Roosevelt's administration, and emerged in the Taft years as full-blown insurgents. Others entered the "progressive" phase of their careers as state politicians. The most famous of these was Robert La Follette, who entered the Senate in 1906 after three terms as the reform Governor of Wisconsin. Albert Cummins of Iowa and Coe Crawford of South Dakota made similar moves in 1909.

Even where the congressional insurgents had played no direct role in state reform movements, the links between progressive Republican movements in the states and Republican insurgency in Congress were usually close. Admittedly, a few insurgents such as William Borah of Idaho and Albert Beveridge of Indiana represented states where Republican progressivism was relatively weak. However, the states that sent large numbers of insurgents to Congress were invariably dominated at home by powerful progressive Republican organizations.

Such states were to be found in two main regions — the Pacific coast and the middle west. "Midwestern" however, is an inadequate term to describe the major area of progressive Republican strength, for the movement was not strong in the more urban, easterly states of the Mississippi valley like Ohio, Michigan, and Illinois. It was rooted rather in a group of agrarian states in the north-central region of the United States — Wisconsin, Minnesota, Iowa, Kansas, Nebraska, and the Dakotas.

In these states a growing demand for reform in the early twentieth century coincided with a tradition of Republican one-party rule. Twenty years before the election of President Taft, the midwestern states which were later to become hotbeds of Republican insurgency had all supported Benjamin Harrison in his narrow victory over Grover Cleveland. In the same year, all five states (the Dakotas were still territories in 1888) had elected Republican Governors and Republican majorities to both houses of their state legislatures. Thirty-one of their thirty-five Congressmen were Republicans, though the G.O.P. had an overall margin in the House of only seven. The smashing Democratic victories of 1890 and 1892 and the Bryan tide in the prairie states temporarily upset the Republicans' hegemony in the early 1890's, but by 1898 the earlier pattern had been restored everywhere. Of the 39 Congressmen from these states in that year, 38 were Republicans, though the party's majority in the House was only 185 to 163.[4] This overwhelming Republican dominance remained unbroken through the next ten years.

In states with well-developed two-party systems, the trend away from conservatism after 1900 was often reflected in a swing toward the Democratic party. But in these one-party states the rising demand for progressive reform produced instead a transformation of the dominant party itself. The very fact that the fruits of office were, as a rule, available only to Republicans in these states encouraged intraparty factionalism. In many cases, prominent insurgents had fallen out with the

---

[4] The election statistics cited above are derived from the *Chicago Daily News Almanac and Yearbook* for the relevant years.

party's leadership over a nomination or a question of patronage long before they became committed to a program of reform. Men like Albert Cummins in Iowa and Coe Crawford in South Dakota had been seeking political office for years before a new political mood developed in the first decade of the twentieth century and enabled them to defeat their opponents under the banner of reform.

As a vehicle for progressive reform at the state level, the Republican party proved as useful an instrument as any other, or so the experience of La Follette, Cummins, Hiram Johnson, and others would suggest. But in national politics the progressive Republicans were successful only insofar as their efforts represented a defensive, regional reaction to the policies of the national party leadership. To some degree, and for some individuals in particular, the Republican insurgency of the Taft years was primarily of this defensive character. The policies of President Taft and the Republican Old Guard after 1909 threatened disaster to the party in the agrarian midwest. Many Republican officeholders, though they were not enthusiastic about progressive reform in general and deplored the split which was developing in the party, felt obliged to go along with the insurgents in order to avoid a Democratic sweep in their home districts. To the extent that sheer self-preservation was their purpose, the insurgents of the Taft years were reasonably successful, for the Democratic victories of 1910 and 1912 did not shake the Republican ascendancy in states like Iowa and Wisconsin as they had done in the 1890's.

Most of the insurgents of the Taft years, however, were not content merely to fight a rear-guard action against the standpat majority of their own party, as conservative Democrats from the south were to resist the liberal majority of their party in the late 1930's. Like the southern Democrats of the later period, the insurgent Republicans of the Taft years had a more powerful grip on their one-party states than their national party had on the national electorate; and like that other minority group, they often held a strategic balance of power in Congress. Unlike the southerners in the latter days of the New Deal, however, there was nothing defensive about the attitude of leading Republican insurgents under Taft and Wilson. On the contrary, they were imbued with the idea, in La Follette's words, that they "could do nationally with the Republican party what we did with it in Wisconsin." [5] Fired with the enthusiasm of reformers and inspired by progressive Republican successes in the states, they set out to win control of the national Republican party and of the federal government. Looking back to the presidency of Theodore Roosevelt, they saw no reason why another progressive Republican should not be elevated to the White House. Indeed the number of presidential hopefuls produced from the progressive Republican ranks is quite remarkable considering the size of the group. La Follette, Cummins, Borah, and Hiram Johnson were all considered serious prospects at one time or another.

In the meantime, however, the insurgents had to face the fact that in national politics they constituted a small "radical" minority in a predominantly conservative party. Somehow they had to find the means of converting this minority into a majority or else find some new political alignment by which they could achieve their ends. It was the tragedy of the Republican insurgents that they never did discover a method of accomplishing what they had set out to do, either inside or outside the Republican party.

The word "insurgent" suggests a mode of political behavior, whereas "progressive" describes, or purports to describe, an ideology; but in practice the two terms can be applied more or less interchangeably to the dissident Republican Congressmen and Senators of the Taft and Wilson years. Admittedly, the insurgent faction in Congress was joined on occasion by men who could hardly be described as progressives, however broadly that vague word were to be defined. Senator Knute Nelson of Minnesota, for instance, took an "insurgent" position on the Payne-Aldrich tariff bill of 1909 but was thoroughly conservative on most issues.[6] There were also Republicans like Senator Dixon of Montana, who deliberately sought middle

[5] Robert M. La Follette, *La Follette's Autobiography* (Madison, Wis., 1911, 1960), p. 320. Page references are to the 1960 edition.
[6] *La Follette's Weekly*, IV, No. 35, August 31, 1912.

positions between the regular and insurgent factions in Congress, or like Senator Bourne of Oregon, whose interest in progressive reform was confined to one particular issue — in Bourne's case "direct democracy" via primary elections.[7] Men like Nelson, Bourne, and Dixon, however, made only sporadic appearances in the insurgent ranks. The hard core of the insurgent faction consisted of men who styled themselves as progressive Republicans and who were committed to a broad range of reform measures.

For the most part, the insurgents represented a rural, traditional brand of progressivism.[8] The centers of insurgent strength were overwhelmingly rural in character, and the insurgents were great exponents of the values of rural life. If there was no hope of relieving "the congested conditions" that existed in the great cities of America, Borah declared on one occasion, "this government would not endure 50 years." It was only because of "the supply of brain and brawn and muscle and manhood and citizenship" coming from "the great rural precincts of the country that we feel safe as to the future of the Republic." [9] George Norris was perturbed by the evidence of the census reports that the cities were growing while the rural areas were losing population. "We ought to legislate so that the reverse would be true. The overcrowded city has always been the breeding place of crime and immorality. The slums of the cities are the places where the anarchist thrives and where there is a lack not only of patriotism for the country, but a lack of morality, of honesty, and of respectability." [10] Senator Clapp thought that the tendency of people to crowd into cities was the greatest menace faced by civilization.[11]

---

[7] For a discussion of Bourne's progressivism, see Albert Heisey Pike Jr., *Jonathan Bourne Jr., Progressive,* unpublished Ph.D. dissertation, University of Oregon, 1957, p. 127.

[8] See John Braeman, "Seven Progressives," *Business History Review,* XXXV (Winter 1961) for a discussion of "moderns" and "traditionalists" among progressives.

[9] *Congressional Record,* 63 Cong., 2 Session, Jan. 15, 1914, p. 1711.

[10] George W. Norris to H. A. Bereman, May 30, 1912, George W. Norris Papers, Library of Congress.

[11] *Cong. Record,* 63 Cong., 2 Session, Feb. 6, 1914, p. 3033.

The insurgents' views on the great national questions of the period reflected their rural, small-town orientation. They were not particularly interested, for instance, in social reforms such as minimum wage and maximum hours legislation, old age pensions, and workmen's compensation, which were chiefly of interest to city workers. It was not so much that they opposed these measures, but just that they paid them little attention. La Follette, perhaps the most radical of the insurgents, showed some interest in welfare programs aimed directly at easing the burdens of underprivileged groups, and allowed labor leaders and social reformers to use *La Follette's Magazine* as a forum for the discussion of social reforms. However, he rarely discussed such matters himself in the signed editorials which dominated the publication. It was typical of La Follette's thinking that he should blame the unemployment of 1913–1914 on a deliberate plot of employers to destroy public confidence in President Wilson's reform program.[12] Since this and other similar social problems were interpreted as further abuses of the corporate power which was the center of the insurgents' concern, the logical solution lay in the destruction or limitation of that power, not in a direct assault on the social problem itself.

In this context it is interesting to note the attitude of the insurgents to the question of taxation. Without any important exception they favored the imposition of graduated federal income and inheritance taxes, and in 1913 they played an important role in the enactment of such a tax program. Historians have hailed this achievement as one of the most important advances of the whole progressive era, without which, as George Mowry has written, it is difficult to see how "most of the social legislation passed since 1912, could have been financed." [13] Although this is a fair comment, it is important to note that few of the insurgents or their allies in the Democratic party were thinking of the great spending programs which Professor Mowry had in mind when they proposed these

---

[12] *La Follette's Weekly,* VI, No. 2, Jan. 10, 1914.
[13] George E. Mowry, *The Era of Theodore Roosevelt and the Birth of Modern America* (New York, 1958), p. 263.

taxes. Their concern was not with revenue but with the re-distribution of wealth and the equalization of burdens. Unlike the urban-oriented liberals of more recent times, they had no great spending programs to finance. Even a man like William Allen White, who by 1912 had become an advocate of some rather advanced programs of social legislation, offered no other outlet for the revenue that higher taxes would produce than "internal improvements under expert direction." [14]

On the positive side, the insurgents were chiefly interested in two main areas of reform: first, the control or the destruction of those iniquitous corporate interests that they variously re-ferred to as "the trusts," "the money power," "the invisible government," or simply "the interests"; second, the extension of "popular government" via such techniques as the direct pri-mary election, women's suffrage, the direct election of Sena-tors, and sometimes the initiative, referendum, and recall. These two issues were closely related in the view of the in-surgents, since they conceived of the politics of the day as a great battle between "the people" and "the interests." It fol-lowed that the extension of the people's rule would automati-cally weaken the malign influence of the corporate interests.

The insurgents blamed clandestine private interests for prac-tically every important inequity in contemporary American life. These included the growing concentration of industry and commerce, the rising cost of living, the corruption of politics, the misuse of the nation's natural resources, and many others. It became almost a mental habit to explain all problems in terms of conspiracies of private wealth. For instance, the in-surgent Congressman Miles Poindexter explained the un-friendly attitude of a conservative newspaper with the casual observation that "undoubtedly an ulterior influence could readily be discovered if an examination was made." [15] When the insurgents were divided on an issue, they sometimes pro-duced such ulterior influences on both sides of the question.

---

[14] William Allen White to James Bryce, Feb. 19, 1917, William Allen White Papers, Library of Congress.

[15] Miles Poindexter to Rufus Rockwell Wilson, Oct. 13, 1909, Miles Poindexter Papers, University of Virginia, Charlottesville, Virginia.

For instance, in 1914 Senator Bristow of Kansas attacked the repeal of the Panama Canal tolls on foreign shipping as a plot of the railroad interests.[16] Senator Kenyon, on the other hand, argued that the tolls ought to be repealed in order that the shipping interests not be unfairly favored.[17]

When it came to providing solutions to the problem of monopoly, the insurgents showed that hesitant approach which Richard Hofstadter has suggested was characteristic of the progressives' attitude to the trusts in general. Albert Cummins, for example, once boldly declared that he favored limiting any trust to 25 percent of the business of a single industry, but then he added lamely, ". . . If there was any effective method by which it could be accomplished." [18]

One solution to the problem of private power would obviously have been to replace it with public power in the form of government ownership. In some specific instances, the insurgents were prepared to embrace such a solution. They supported, for instance, government-owned coal mines and railroads in Alaska and a government-owned shipping line to meet the transportation difficulties caused by the World War. But there were severe limits to how far they were prepared to go with state ownership, implying as it did a radical threat to property rights. State socialism, the insurgents believed, was not the solution to private monopoly, but another malignant threat to American liberty.

Graduated income and inheritance taxes were other possible ways of attacking privileged minorities, and the progressive Republicans were certainly strong advocates of these. But even in their advocacy of graduated taxation, their reluctance to appear as enemies of property was very clear. Of the insurgents who spoke on the issue in the Senate debates of 1913, only George Norris spoke openly of the need "to break up the swollen fortunes." [19] The others went out of their way to deny that they had any such idea in mind. The income tax amend-

[16] *Cong. Record,* 63 Cong., 2 Session, Feb. 18, 1914, p. 3599.

[17] *Ibid.,* May 20, 1914, p. 8887.

[18] *Ibid.,* 63 Cong., 1 Session, August 29, 1913, p. 3862.

[19] *Ibid.,* Sept. 8, 1913, p. 4436.

ment proposed by Bristow was, according to Cummins, "a very moderate, conservative, suggestion." [20] It was not intended, according to Borah, "to equalize the fortunes of this country through taxation." [21] Their purpose, the insurgents declared, was merely to share the tax burden more fairly. Even Norris was moved to deny at one point that he had any "disposition to legislate against or to criticize the man who is getting a large income." [22]

If the insurgents can be said to have held any particular view of the trust problem, it was the direct antithesis of Theodore Roosevelt's belief that industrial combinations were "the result of an imperative economic law," the answer to which lay "not in attempting to prevent such combinations but in completely controlling them in the interest of the public welfare." [23] Beveridge was the only important insurgent leader to hold such "New Nationalist" views. The others took the contrary position that combinations and monopolies arose from the exercise of special privileges and unlawful practices in business and politics. The solution therefore lay in the abolition of unfair and unlawful business practices and political privileges. Some of the insurgents, such as Senator Bristow, moved toward Roosevelt's view of the trust question around 1911 and 1912 when they found their political fortunes becoming closely tied to his.[24] But on the whole Roosevelt had surprisingly little influence on the insurgents' attitude towards the trusts. Men like Senator Borah went right on denouncing trust-regulation schemes at the very moment when they were endorsing Roosevelt for President in 1912.

Though the insurgents were on the whole agreed that the trusts ought to be destroyed rather than regulated, they were

[20] *Ibid.*, August 27, 1913, p. 3817.
[21] *Ibid.*, August 27, 1913, p. 3807.
[22] *Ibid.*, August 27, 1913, p. 3809.
[23] Theodore Roosevelt, *The New Nationalism,* ed. William E. Leuchtenburg (Englewood Cliffs, N.J., 1961), p. 29.
[24] For Bristow's change of opinion on the trust question compare Joseph L. Bristow to William Allen White, Jan. 11, 1912, Joseph L. Bristow Papers, Kansas State Historical Society, Topeka, Kansas; and Bristow to Theodore Roosevelt, July 15, 1912, *ibid.*

still divided as to how this could best be done. Borah believed that little or no additional government machinery was necessary to police the economy against combinations in restraint of trade. All that was necessary was for the Attorney General to enforce the Sherman Anti-trust Act effectively, together with the enactment of some supplementary laws to outlaw certain specific trade practices and to provide stiffer penalties for corporation officers who broke the law. The whole problem of the trusts boiled down, in Borah's view, to the activities of a few dishonest individuals, possibly as few as 300 in the United States.[25] Borah's position was backed by the more conservative insurgents, such as Senators Sterling of South Dakota and Works of California, who feared the power of the federal government almost as much as they feared the trusts and who opposed the establishment of new federal agencies to cope with the problem.

Another position was taken by Senator Cummins, one of the authors of the Federal Trade Commission Act of 1914. Cummins agreed with Borah that it would be helpful to outlaw as many unfair trade practices as possible and to make corporation officials personally responsible for the policies of their firms. But he believed that the Attorney General could not carry out these laws effectively, and he favored the setting up of a Federal Commission modeled on the Interstate Commerce Commission, equipped with broad powers. When the Federal Trade Commission was established in 1914, its critics, including Borah, charged that this step marked the beginning of trust regulation in the United States, a belief that recent historians have endorsed.[26] But Cummins denied that the Act had any such purpose. The commission, he said, was designed to suppress unfair competition, and by doing so, would destroy the very means by which monopoly was established.[27]

The insurgents' rejection of Theodore Roosevelt's "New Nationalist" approach to the leading domestic issue of the day

---

[25] *Cong. Record,* 63 Cong., 2 Session, Sept. 30, 1914, p. 15949.

[26] Arthur S. Link, *Woodrow Wilson and the Progressive Era* (New York, 1954), p. 74.

[27] *Cong. Record,* 63 Cong., 2 Session, July 29, 1914, p. 12919.

went largely unnoticed at the time, but the ideological void which separated the midwestern insurgents from Roosevelt's brand of progressivism became clear after 1914, when international issues began to impinge on American politics. In these years President Wilson's handling of the difficult problems raised by the revolution in Mexico and the World War in Europe came under fire from two sides. On the one hand were militants who favored stronger action against Mexico and Germany, and on the other were pacifists who believed Wilson was already acting too aggressively on both fronts. Though Theodore Roosevelt soon emerged as America's number one militant on these international issues, the great majority of the insurgents took the opposite point of view. Among the Senate insurgents, only Borah and Sterling criticized Wilson from something like a militant standpoint. The others were deeply disturbed at the prospect of American intervention in Mexico or Europe, and it was Republican insurgents who formed the backbone of the "little group of willful men" who fought the last battles against American entry to the World War.[28]

While the insurgents' political views may be readily distinguished from those of Theodore Roosevelt and his "New Nationalist" supporters, it would be wrong to look upon insurgency as an ideological position. Not only was there some diversity of opinion in the insurgent ranks, but many of the generalizations that have been made about the insurgents' political attitudes would apply equally well to many Democratic progressives from similar rural backgrounds. What divided the insurgents from these potential allies was not ideology but party affiliation. The insurgents were enthusiastic progressives, but they were also committed Republicans. Their efforts to reconcile these two positions are the subject of this book.

---

[28] For a full account of the progressive Republicans' attitude to the international problems of the Wilson years, see Chapter 9.

# chapter two

# The Struggle with Cannon

In the first two years of the Taft administration, the split which had been developing for some years between progressive and conservative Republicans erupted in a series of violent intraparty battles. Insurgent Republicans in both Houses of Congress launched vigorous attacks on the party's "Old Guard," personified by Nelson W. Aldrich in the Senate and Joseph G. Cannon in the House. In the Senate the first great battle was fought over the Payne-Aldrich tariff bill, which was enacted despite insurgent and Democratic opposition in 1909. The leading issue of the day in the House was the allegedly dictatorial power of Speaker Cannon himself. Here the insurgents won a major victory, combining with the Democratic minority in March 1910 to amend the House Rules so as to reduce the Speaker's powers.

Resentment of the Speaker's great powers in the House did not begin with the Taft administration or even the accession of Joseph Cannon to the office in 1903;[1] anti-"Cannonism" became a significant force only with the rise of the progressive Republican faction in Congress. For instance, the insurgent leader George W. Norris had no objections to the House Rules during his first two terms in Congress.[2] But as Norris and men like him moved left in the latter years of the Roosevelt admin-

---

[1] Kenneth W. Hechler, *Insurgency: Personalities and Politics of the Taft Era* (New York, 1940), pp. 28–30.
[2] Lowitt, *Norris,* pp. 89, 93, 100–101.

istration, they came to view the Speaker and the power he wielded as obstacles to progressive reform. It was not the power of the Speaker itself which provoked the insurgent revolt, but power exercised in the interests of standpat policies.[3]

The first serious moves against Cannon's authority were made during the lame duck session of the Sixtieth Congress, which met in December 1908. A group of 29 Republican insurgents signed a resolution in February 1909 calling for the abolition of the Speaker's power to appoint the standing committees, the institution of a new Rules committee, elected by the House, which would select the standing committees, and the introduction of a monthly "Calendar Tuesday" on which all the committees, in alphabetical order, could present legislation. In an effort to appease the insurgents and to isolate the more radical reformers, the Republican leadership agreed to establish a calendar day much like the one the insurgents had proposed. Most of the insurgents joined the Democrats in condemning this concession as inadequate, but it passed anyway by a narrow margin.[4]

In the Sixty-first Congress, which opened in March 1909, both the Democrats and Republican insurgents were numeri-

---

[3] Hechler, *Insurgency*, p. 31.
[4] This paragraph is a summary of Hechler, *Insurgency*, pp. 44–48. Most of the narrative of the following two paragraphs also follows Hechler.

cally stronger, and the Rules reformers confidently expected to control enough votes to upset the Speaker. Their calculations were upset, however, when the Cannon organization was able to win support from two unexpected sources. First, President Taft, threatened with noncooperation on his legislative program in the House, agreed to use his influence on Republican Congressmen in favor of the regular organization. Then, 23 Democrats led by John J. Fitzgerald refused to follow their own party leadership for reasons of their own and sided with the Republican regulars on the crucial roll calls.[5]

For the remainder of this session of Congress, the Rules issue remained dormant, but the insurgents had not abandoned their cause and were merely waiting for another opportunity to challenge the Speaker. Eventually, in the second session of the Sixty-first Congress, that moment arrived. On March 17, 1910, George Norris, by a clever parliamentary tactic, managed to bring to the floor of the House a resolution to amend the Rules.[6] On this occasion the insurgent-Democratic alliance held firm, and on the final roll call Norris's amendment was adopted by 191 to 156 votes. Forty-two Republican Congressmen joined the minority in opposing their own party's leadership.

The Norris resolution set up a new Rules committee chosen by the House rather than by the Speaker and deprived the Speaker of a seat on the committee. As soon as it was declared carried, Speaker Cannon made a brief statement in which he refused to resign but offered to entertain a resolution declaring the Speaker's office vacant. A Democratic Congressman, Albert Burleson of Texas, accepted the Speaker's challenge, and over the protests of many of his colleagues he did as the Speaker had suggested; but only nine Republican insurgents,

---

[5] Hechler, *Insurgency,* pp. 49–58.

[6] See Hechler, *Insurgency,* pp. 67–78; Lowitt, *Norris,* pp. 166–182; George E. Mowry, *Theodore Roosevelt and the Progressive Movement* (Madison, Wis., 1946), pp. 91–93; Blair Bolles, *Tyrant from Illinois: Uncle Joe Cannon's Experiment with Personal Power* (New York, 1951), pp. 215–224; William Rea Gwinn, *Uncle Joe Cannon, Archfoe of Insurgency* (New York, 1957), pp. 206–216.

led by Victor Murdock of Kansas, voted for Burleson's resolution. The others took Norris's lead and voted with the regulars to keep Cannon in the chair.

The defeat of the powerful Speaker was certainly a major victory for the small group of insurgent Republicans in the House, but how much they really gained from their victory is questionable. Norris believed that "the overthrow of the political oligarchy known as 'Cannonism' in the Republican machine, did accomplish a great step forward in the right direction. . . . There is a new atmosphere in the House of Representatives. There is more independence than there ever has been." [7] Perhaps minority groups in the House like the Republican insurgents benefited somewhat from the decentralization of the Speaker's powers under the new Rules, but fundamentally their legislative influence was no greater after the Rules battle than it had been before. The insurgents not only allowed Cannon to remain in the Chair by voting against the Burleson resolution, but also made no attempt to influence the composition of the new Rules committee, allowing the regulars to fill all the Republican positions without opposition.[8] Thus the power wrested from the Speaker merely passed into the hands of the collective Republican leadership — a group no more inclined toward progressive policies than Cannon himself.

Why did the insurgents fail to press for more tangible results from the Rules victory than that "new atmosphere" alluded to by Norris? For one thing, their ideological preoccupation with the evils of machine controls led them to overestimate the importance of their victory. Underlying all the attacks made by the progressive Republicans on "Cannonism" and "Aldrichism" ran the assumption that political machines were invariably allies of "the interests" and enemies of progressivism. Conversely, a true progressive must be, *ipso facto*, independent of political machines. For instance, to support their assertion that the Democrats were not progressives, they

[7] Norris to A. C. Rankin, March 21, 1912, Norris Papers.
[8] New York *Times,* March 21, 1910; *ibid.,* March 24, 1910.

cited, not Democratic voting records on progressive issues, but
the fact that Democratic Congressmen were "slaves of the party
caucus." "The progressive and independent members are confined almost entirely to the Republican party in the House of
Representatives," Norris once remarked;[9] and since these two
qualities — progressivism and independence — were inextrica-
bly bound together, it followed that the destruction of the
Cannon organization in the House must in the long run advance the progressive cause, even if the immediate benefits
were not readily apparent.

It was this view of conservatism as the product of special
interests working through political machines that enabled the
insurgents to convince themselves that they, and not the more
numerous regular Republicans, truly represented the ordinary
party supporter. "We took another licking yesterday, but there
were some twenty Republicans who had backbone enough to
stand out against the machine," the Wisconsin insurgent Irvine Lenroot wrote in April 1909. "If I thought the Republican organization under the dome of the Capitol represented
the Republican party of this country, I would be ashamed of
being a Republican, but knowing that it does not, I believe
that it is only a question of a short time until the rank and
file of the Republican party will control Congress." [10] In Lenroot's view then, only 20 insurgents represented the Republican rank and file, and he implied that it was solely fear of the
machine that kept the other 200 Republican Representatives
in the conservative camp. Once this machine control broke
down the insurgents were confident that the true progressive
nature of the Republican party would shine forth. There were
"a few ingrained Tories" in the party, Miles Poindexter admitted, but "the great forward movement of the Republican
party will probably leave . . . [the conservatives] either entirely without a party or else they will take refuge in the

---

[9] Norris to I. D. Evans, June 23, 1911, Norris Papers.
[10] Irvine Lenroot to Nils P. Haugen, April 6, 1909, Nils P. Haugen
Papers, State Historical Society of Wisconsin, Madison, Wisconsin.

Democratic party." [11] Overthrowing Cannon on the Rules was to be a first step in the forward movement.

The insurgents had other more practical reasons for restricting their efforts to a revision of the Rules. Publicly, the majority of the insurgents who had voted against the Burleson resolution argued that they had done so to prove that they were standing for a principle and that they would not injure the principle for the gratification of any personal vengeance.[12] Also, Norris argued, it would make little difference who was Speaker if the desired changes in the Rules were made.[13] But despite their protests the insurgents were not really disinterested in the question of who occupied the Speaker's chair. It took more resolution to vote for Cannon, Norris admitted, than any other vote of his career.[14] The insurgents would have liked nothing better than to have placed in the Speaker's office a man "more in harmony with . . . the great spirit of reform which is pervading the entire country," as Poindexter put it.[15] And Norris had no objection to ousting Cannon if the deed could be done within the Republican caucus.[16]

But the insurgents were only a small helpless minority inside the party caucus. Their strength came from the balance of power they held on the floor of the House, where they could only depose the Speaker with the aid of the Democratic minority. Such a step would have been fraught with dangerous possibilities. Having unseated the Speaker the next question would be the choice of his successor. The insurgents might try to force the regulars to accept a compromise candidate on whom both wings of the party could unite, but it was by no means sure that the Republican regulars would surrender to

---

[11] Miles Poindexter to Prof. W. D. Lyman, Oct. 6, 1910, Poindexter Papers; Poindexter to H. Y. Saint, Oct. 7, 1910, *ibid.*
[12] Norris to D. L. Crellin, April 1, 1910, Norris Papers.
[13] Norris to Ernest C. Nyrop, March 4, 1909, *ibid.*
[14] Norris to D. L. Crellin, April 1, 1910, *ibid.*
[15] Poindexter to Norman Hapgood, Nov. 17, 1908, Poindexter Papers.
[16] Norris to Ernest C. Nyrop, March 4, 1909, Norris Papers.

such a small minority of the party. Probably they would vote to re-elect Cannon, and unless the insurgents voted for a Democrat, deadlock would ensue. This would provide an issue on which the insurgents could be attacked. "We cannot afford to be put in the position of defeating the necessary legislation," one insurgent warned. It would be better to "force him [Cannon] to continue to occupy the post of responsibility so that if there is a failure of legislation, blame for it will rest on him, as Speaker, the committees which he appointed, and the committee on Rules all six Republicans of which are his friends." [17]

The alternative of joining the Democrats to elect a Democratic Speaker was equally unpalatable to the insurgents. "I would vote for Cannon before I would cast my vote for any Democrat," Norris stated categorically.[18] To vote with the Democrats on one particular issue was one thing; to join them in organizing the House was quite another, for it implied a permanent realignment of parties in Congress. There did exist, of course, a school of thought that saw party realignment on an ideological basis as highly desirable,[19] but no office-holding insurgent Republican took such a view. Coming as most of them did from Republican-dominated states, they had no wish to court political destruction by losing their identity as Republicans. They did not fear to attack Cannon from within the party. Indeed their constituents encouraged them to do so. ". . . the more you can 'insurge' the stronger will be your hold here at home," a Wisconsin insurgent was assured by a sympathetic state legislator.[20] But the insurgents could have no assurance that anti-Cannon sentiment was strong enough to sustain a complete break with traditional party loyalties. In any case the partisanship of most of the insur-

[17] James H. Davidson to John J. Esch, April 16, 1910, John J. Esch Papers, State Historical Society of Wisconsin, Madison, Wisconsin.
[18] Norris to Adam Breade, June 4, 1909, Norris Papers.
[19] See, for instance, Henry Wallace to Jonathan P. Dolliver, Sept. 23, 1909, Jonathan P. Dolliver Papers, Iowa State Historical Society, Iowa City, Iowa.
[20] Merlin Hull to John J. Esch, June 17, 1909, Esch Papers.

gents was as deep-dyed as that of their constituents. The Democrats had only joined them in the fight against Cannon, they argued, for reasons of political expediency. In Norris's opinion the Democrats in the House had more in common with the Republican regulars than they had with the insurgents.[21] Robert La Follette characterized the Democratic strategy in Congress at this time as "partisan rather than progressive." [22] The Democracy used to be called the Bourbon Democracy, Poindexter recalled, because Democrats, like Louis XVI, were standpatters.[23]

Fear of becoming too closely tied to the Democrats was the major reason why the insurgents decided not to press for representation on the new Rules committee. "What makes them hesitate to assume a strategic position from which they might dominate the new committee," one correspondent noted, "is just the fear that at every crisis the question would be put squarely to them again to ally themselves with the Democrats for the defeat of their own party's plans." [24] In order to avoid this kind of embarrassment, the insurgents preferred to keep Cannon in the chair and regulars on the Rules committee. It was much safer, one insurgent confided to a colleague, "to keep the responsibility on the old crowd." [25]

Thus the insurgents voted against Burleson's resolution and decided not to press for representation on the Rules committee, partly because they believed the revision of the Rules was itself a significant victory, partly to avoid responsibility for a legislative deadlock, and perhaps most important of all, because they wished to demonstrate that their liaison with the Democrats was no more than a temporary affair of convenience. Progressive control of the Republican party, not a bipartisan alliance, was the insurgent goal. "I believe that the only permanent relief that can come to the country," Norris wrote in 1911, "is from the progressive wing of the Republican

---

[21] Norris to Will Owen Jones, Sept. 13, 1910. Norris Papers.
[22] La Follette, *Autobiography* (Madison, Wis., 1911, 1960), p. 318.
[23] Poindexter to W. D. Smith, Jan. 24, 1910. Poindexter Papers.
[24] New York *Times,* March 21, 1910.
[25] James H. Davidson to John J. Esch, March 26, 1910, Esch Papers.

party." [26] The whole range of progressive-conservative issues, the insurgents hoped, could be confined to an intraparty struggle between Republicans, with the Democrats relegated to the wings.

This strategy, which had worked so well in one-party states like Iowa and Kansas, was doomed to failure in national two-party politics. The insurgents could save their identification as Republicans by voting against Burleson's resolution and limiting cooperation with the Democrats to a few specific issues, but they could not insulate the battle over Cannonism from the two-party contest. The immediate political effect of the progressive Republican assaults on "Cannonism" in the House and "Aldrichism" in the Senate was to raise the prestige of the insurgents at the expense of the Old Guard. The further effect was, however, not to deliver the Republican party into the hands of the progressives, but to put national power in the hands of the Democrats. In the midterm elections of 1910 the progressive Republicans succeeded in consolidating their control of the north-central states of the country, but on a national scale it was the Democrats who triumphed, taking control of the House of Representatives for the first time since 1892. The politics of Iowa and Kansas could not so simply be transplanted in Washington.

There was one way in which the Republican insurgents might have emerged substantially more powerful from the battle over the Rules. Had the Republican leadership in the House been willing to compromise with the progressive Republicans in order to maintain party unity, the insurgents would have achieved a greater measure of legislative influence without being forced into an unwanted alliance with the Democrats. Some of the Old Guard leaders were apparently anxious to establish such unity and might have been prepared to make real legislative concessions. For instance, Sereno Payne, chairman of the House Ways and Means committee, issued a statement after the Rules fight stating that the Rules

---

[26] Norris to I. D. Evans, June 23, 1911, Norris Papers.

issue having been settled, House Republicans would hence-forth remain united on all other major questions.[27]

But another very different mood was current among con-servative Republicans during the years of insurgency, and it proved to be the dominant one in all moments of crisis. This was the view that the progressive Republicans were more dan-gerous than the Democrats and ought to be driven out of the party even at the cost of a party split and a Democratic vic-tory. Like the insurgents, standpat Republicans had few doubts about the righteousness of their policies and the in-evitability of their continuance in power in the long run. Though the Democrats might win an occasional election, their unsound views on the tariff question or on monetary policy would be bound to lead to disaster as they had done in Cleve-land's time, and the Grand Old Party would then return to pick up the reins of power that rightfully belonged to it. But if radicalism took over the Republican party, it was an alto-gether more serious matter. Then there would be no safe re-pository for "sound policies," and the welfare of the Republic might be in serious danger. Consequently it was much better to stand rigidly for traditional conservative doctrines and fight to keep the party organization safe from insurgent control than to compromise with the reformers in the hope of imme-diate electoral success. Views such as these run through the private correspondence of standpat Republicans in the years of the insurgent revolt.[28]

No one stood more firmly for uncompromising resistance to progressivism in the Republican party than Joseph G. Can-

---

[27] New York *Times,* March 20, 1910.

[28] N. D. Pratt to George D. Perkins, Feb. 6, 1911, George D. Perkins Papers, Iowa State Department of History and Archives, Des Moines, Iowa; C. W. Johnson to Perkins, July 30, 1910, *ibid.;* Ellsworth Rominger to John F. Lacey, Feb. 12, 1910, John F. Lacey Papers, Iowa State Department of History and Archives, Des Moines, Iowa; J. S. Bellamy to Lacey, July 18, 1910, *ibid.;* Herman P. Goebel to James A. Tawney, Sept. 27, 1910, James A. Tawney Papers, Minne-sota Historical Society, St. Paul, Minnesota.

non himself. After his defeat on the Rules issue, Cannon refused to make peace with the insurgents but rather attacked them vigorously and repeatedly in a series of public addresses. Historians have generally interpreted these speeches of Cannon's as the irrational, vindictive attacks of an embittered old man. No doubt Cannon was motivated in part by a desire to get even with those who had humiliated him, but he would never have agreed with the early historian who wrote of this period that "the situation in general clearly demanded a policy of conciliation and mutual concessions." [29] Cannon saw no virtue in a "nominal Republican majority made up of 'guerillas' who serve in either army as they can make their bargains." [30] In November 1909 he declared that he knew only one way to treat the insurgents and that was "to fight them just as we fight Mr. Bryan and his following." [31] To have compromised with the insurgents in order to achieve a united party would have been a Pyrrhic victory in the Speaker's view. "We had better fight and fall standing by Republican policies," he advised a fellow standpatter, "than to fight and win and have victory, like Dead Sea fruit, turn to ashes on our lips." [32] The proper policy in Cannon's view was to keep the Grand Old Party intact and to force the insurgents to admit that they were really Democrats in disguise.

It was with this aim in mind that Cannon, after his defeat on the Rules, invited the insurgent-Democratic coalition to declare the Speaker's office vacant and choose a new Speaker representing "the Democratic and insurgent Members, who by their last vote, evidently constitute a majority of this House." [33] The result was the Burleson resolution and the re-election of Cannon to his office with the substantial help of insurgent votes. In the months that followed Cannon pressed ahead with

---

[29] Charles R. Atkinson, *The Committee on Rules and the Overthrow of Speaker Cannon* (New York, 1911), p. 126.

[30] Joseph G. Cannon to Charles D. Norton, July 21, 1910. William Howard Taft Papers, Library of Congress.

[31] New York *Times,* Nov. 27, 1909.

[32] Cannon to George D. Perkins, March 22, 1910, Perkins Papers.

[33] *Cong. Record,* 61 Cong., 2 Session, March 19, 1910, p. 3437.

the same policy. He attacked the insurgents for not having the courage of their convictions and failing to stick to their new alliance. The Republican party did not really have a majority in the House, Cannon said, because some so-called Republicans were really Populists, attempting to outdo Bryanism.[34]

To bolster his argument that the insurgents were not really Republicans at all, Cannon produced a whole theory of political parties on which he expounded at length during his dramatic speech in the House. "This is a government," Cannon said, "by the people acting through the representatives of a majority of the people." Effective government depended on the majority having full power to govern and the existence of a minority ever ready to take advantage of the majority's mistakes. There was a widespread belief, Cannon went on, that the Republican party had a majority of 44 in the House of Representatives, but this was a misconception. In fact, "the minority, supplemented by the efforts of the so-called insurgents, constituting 15 per cent of the majority party in the House," was the real majority. "There has been much talk on the part of the minority and the insurgents of the "Czarism" of the Speaker, culminating in the action taken today. The real truth is that there is no coherent Republican majority in the House of Representatives. Therefore the real majority ought to have the courage of its convictions and logically meet the situation which confronts it." [35]

It is a tribute to the imaginative powers of the Speaker, or whoever wrote his speech, that he should have produced at this moment of crisis a theory of congressional parties that bore so little resemblance to the realities of American politics. Cannon's picture of a new majority coalition coming to power after the defeat of the old majority on a single major issue would have made excellent sense if he had been speaking of the British parliament, but it had no relevance to the situation in the United States Congress. It was fruitless for Cannon to protest that the Republican insurgents had, by their vote

---

[34] New York *Times,* March 21, 1910; *ibid.,* May 1, 1910.
[35] *Cong. Record,* 61 Cong., 2 Session, March 19, 1910, pp. 3436–3437.

on the Rules, joined the opposition party. Only in a parliamentary system, where the very stability of the executive branch depends on the continuous support of a legislative majority, can insurgency and nonparty voting be outlawed in this way. The House insurgents were certainly not bound to choose between their own party and the opposition. And in truth Cannon did not follow his own rules on party voting, since, as the insurgents were quick to point out, he had always been perfectly willing to trade votes with the Democratic leadership when it had suited his purpose.[36]

In the short run Cannon's attacks on the insurgents could do them little harm. He could not force them to form a permanent alliance with the Democrats if they did not choose to do so. Nor could he weaken them substantially in their home states by accusing them of "un-Republicanism" for paradoxically, it was precisely in these one-party Republican-dominated states of the agricultural middle west that the reaction against Cannonism benefited insurgent Republicans rather than Democrats.

Nevertheless, the challenge which Cannon offered the Republican insurgents in 1910 was in the last analysis a real one. For by branding them as Democrats and refusing to cooperate or compromise with them, Cannon had touched upon the insurgents' weakest spot. If the conservatives of their own party refused to budge under their pressure and a permanent alliance with the Democrats was ruled out, how were the progressive Republicans to advance their cause? In 1912 the question was to be put to them again in an even more poignant form.

---

[36] Joseph L. Bristow to A. C. Mitchell, Oct. 18, 1909. Bristow Papers.

# chapter three

# Insurgency at High Tide

The Payne-Aldrich tariff bill was to the progressive Republicans of the Senate what Cannon and the Rules were to the House insurgents. The bill had its immediate origins in the Republican party platform of 1908, which had included a plank calling for tariff revision. Though the platform was not explicit on the point, it was generally assumed that the Republican party had thereby committed itself to a downward revision of the existing tariff rates, and it was to fulfil this pledge that President Taft called Congress into special session in March 1909. A few days after the opening of the session, the tariff bill was introduced to the House by Sereno Payne, chairman of the Ways and Means committee, where it was passed on April 9 by a party vote.[1]

But in the Senate, the tariff bill of 1909 ran into serious opposition from dissident Republicans, provoked some of the hottest congressional debates of modern times, and brought about an open party split. The bill which Aldrich reported to the Senate on April 12 contained several hundred amendments to the rates set by the House, most of them upward, and deleted the House version's provision for an inheritance tax. All over the country public reaction to Aldrich's bill was extremely hostile, for it was widely believed that high tariff rates fostered monopolies and were responsible for the rising

---

[1] Full accounts of the Payne-Aldrich tariff dispute may be found in Mowry, *Theodore Roosevelt and the Progressive Movement,* pp. 46–65; and Hechler, *Insurgency,* pp. 92–145.

cost of living.[2] Besides, Aldrich seemed to have no regard for public opinion or his party's pledges, even denying at one point that the Republicans were committed to downward revision.[3]

A group of insurgent Republican Senators refused to go along with Aldrich's tariff bill and joined the Democrats in a long and bitter fight against its key schedules during the spring and summer of 1909.[4] The exact number of tariff insurgents varied from one moment to another, but on the final roll call ten Republican Senators voted against the bill. These were Cummins and Dolliver of Iowa, Clapp and Nelson of Minnesota, Brown and Burkett of Nebraska, La Follette of Wisconsin, Bristow of Kansas, Beveridge of Indiana, and Crawford of South Dakota. Of this group, those Senators who cannot be clearly identified as "progressives"—Nelson, Burkett, and Brown—all came from states where the progressive Republican movement was very powerful.[5]

There were many parallels between insurgency in the Senate and the House. Senate insurgency, like its counterpart in the House, was an organized, disciplined force. The Senate insurgents divided the various schedules of the tariff amongst themselves for study purposes so that each man could bring as much expertise as possible to the debates, and they met together from time to time to coordinate their legislative

---

[2] See New York *Times,* Feb. 11, 1910, and March 24, 1910, for the extent of public hostility to the Payne-Aldrich tariff.

[3] New York *Times,* April 23, 1909.

[4] Besides the works mentioned in note 1, see George E. Mowry, *Era of Theodore Roosevelt,* pp. 242–247; Ross, *Dolliver,* pp. 237–264; Bowers, *Beveridge,* pp. 333–366; La Follette, *La Follette,* pp. 272–278.

[5] Knute Nelson was the most obvious nonprogressive among the tariff insurgents. See, for instance, La Follette's attack on Nelson as a "system Senator" in *La Follette's Weekly,* IV, No. 35, August 31, 1912. Brown and Burkett are less easily classified. George Norris, who defeated Brown in a senatorial primary in 1912, and who considered running against Burkett in 1910, did not consider either man a progressive. See Norris to Ray McCarl, July 10, 1911, Norris Papers; also Lowitt, *Norris,* pp. 190, 192.

strategy. Like the House insurgents again, the Senate rebels turned their attack directly on the Republican leadership in Congress, having much to say about the motives and legislative methods of Senator Aldrich and his lieutenants. For instance, Dolliver's great speech of May 4 was characterized by one correspondent as "the frankest raking over heard in the Senate in many a day." Dolliver, he noted, while attacking the tariff bill, "its makers, and the manner of its making" had returned again and again to phrases such as "slippery places," "tricks," "misleading language," and even the unparliamentary "dishonest." [6] La Follette's biographers note that during the tariff debates he "lost no opportunity to fix responsibility for increased tariff duties upon Aldrich and his associates." [7]

The response of the standpat Republican leadership in the Senate to the insurgent attacks was as uncompromising as Cannon's. Senator Aldrich, it is true, did not face exactly the same problem as his opposite number in the House, since on most of the crucial divisions he controlled enough votes to defeat the insurgent-Democratic alliance. Yet the public reaction to the tariff bill was so adverse and the attacks of the dissident Republican Senators so bitter that one might have expected the Senatorial Old Guard to have followed a conciliatory policy in order to appease the critics and maintain a semblance of party unity. Except for one half-hearted attempt to conciliate the insurgents with a few modest reductions, Aldrich preferred to stick to his original proposals unless actual defeat threatened on the floor of the Senate.[8] This happened only once, when in order to head off a powerful Democratic-insurgent drive for a graduated income tax amendment to the tariff bill, Aldrich reluctantly agreed to accept a tax on corporations.[9] Otherwise, the Old Guard spurned a policy of unity through concessions, maintained its high tariff position, and attacked the insurgents, in the Cannon manner,

---

[6] New York *Times,* May 5, 1909.

[7] La Follette, *La Follette,* p. 275.

[8] Hechler, *Insurgency,* pp. 114–115.

[9] *Ibid.,* pp. 146–163; Mowry, *Theodore Roosevelt and the Progressive Movement,* pp. 57–58.

as Democrats in disguise. "I say to the Senator from Indiana and to his friends," Aldrich chided Beveridge, "that the Republican party is a party of majorities. . . . The Senator from Indiana does not speak for the Republican party." [10]

Like their brethren in the House, the tariff rebels reacted violently to any aspersions on their Republicanism. They denied that acceptance or nonacceptance of the Senate Finance committee's tariff rates was an adequate test of Republicanism. "I do not think the chairman of the Finance committee has any more authority to say to me that I have no right to speak as a Republican," Senator Crawford complained, "than I have to say the same thing to him." [11] Instead Senator Cummins suggested "the arbiter as to the Republicanism of those who voted against the tariff bill" should be "the national Republican platform of 1908." [12] Cummins was on rather weak ground here for a progressive Republican, since Republican party platforms in general were not notable for their progressive sentiments. Indeed in a few more years Cummins could be heard saying in the Senate, "I am not very solicitous about platforms when it comes to legislation." [13] But in the immediate situation there could be no better defense against Aldrich's charges than an appeal to the platform of 1908.

The "defensive" aspects of insurgency were perhaps more prominent in the Payne-Aldrich affair than in the Cannon fight. By insisting on a high tariff bill in the face of a widespread demand for downward revision, Aldrich not only turned dissident regulars like Dolliver and Beveridge into fullblown insurgents, but also forced moderates like Burkett and conservatives like Nelson temporarily into the insurgent camp. Cannon and Aldrich were burdensome loads for Republican politicians to carry in states like Nebraska and Minnesota, and men of this type apparently felt it necessary to break with the Congressional leadership in order to have any chance of po-

---

[10] *Cong. Record,* 61 Cong., 1 Session, July 8, 1909, p. 4314.
[11] *Ibid.,* p. 4315.
[12] Address to the Marquette Club, Chicago, by Senator Cummins, Nov. 6, 1909, *Senate Document* 204, 61 Cong., 2 Series, Vol. 58.
[13] *Cong. Record,* 63 Cong., 2 Session, July 29, 1914, p. 12919.

litical survival. Such men, however, were usually careful not to move too far from Republican orthodoxy. Brown and Burkett, for instance, chose to vote for the conference report on the Payne-Aldrich bill, claiming that the conference committee, under President Taft's pressure, had produced a satisfactory bill.[14] In the elections of 1910, Nelson endorsed the candidacy of Congressman Tawney, the Cannon lieutenant who was the only Minnesota representative to vote for the Payne-Aldrich tariff and the man whom President Taft was defending when he made the famous Winona speech.[15]

But there was little real prospect of renewed harmony between the hard-core insurgents and the regular Republican faction in Congress after the great battles over the tariff and the Rules. The insurgents were elated by the success of their efforts to discredit the Old Guard in Congress, and they were all the more determined to push ahead with their own program of progressive reform in the coming sessions. Just one month after the President signed the Payne-Aldrich tariff into law, Bristow was writing to Cummins about a proposed conference of insurgent Senators on the forthcoming railroad legislation. "We should get our friends united on it, consult with each other, and then when you go to Washington in November, start the fight before the President. We will make it first before him, and if we fail, will fight it out in Congress." [16] Three weeks later Cummins was planning to "get some of the boys . . . together at Chicago" before the new session opened, where he hoped Bristow, Beveridge, La Follette, Clapp, Brown, Dolliver, and himself could "spend a few hours together without any publicity." [17]

In line with this strategy, the Senate insurgents struck a blow against the Old Guard in March 1910, with an amendment of Borah's to the Post Office Savings bill. The amendment prohibited the investment of postal savings funds in

---

[14] Albert B. Cummins to Albert J. Beveridge, Sept. 13, 1909, Albert J. Beveridge Papers, Library of Congress.
[15] Knute Nelson to C. L. Swanson, August 31, 1910, Tawney Papers.
[16] Bristow to Cummins, Sept. 7, 1909, Bristow Papers.
[17] Cummins to Bristow, Oct. 1, 1909, *ibid.*

bonds bearing an interest rate of less than two and a half per cent, the effect of which would have been to destroy Aldrich's plan for the investment of the funds in national bank bonds. According to Bristow, this scheme was "the first move in the reorganization of the currency system . . . giving J. P. Morgan and Co. and a few of their financial associates control of the currency. . . . It is the boldest effort yet made in the history of this country to entrench the control and domination of the Government in the hands of a few rich men in New York." [18] The amendment was passed in the Senate by an insurgent-Democratic alliance, but it was cut out of the bill by the conference committee.[19]

However, the progressive Republicans did succeed in leaving a permanent imprint on the railroad legislation of 1910. The legislative history of the Mann-Elkins Act is a complex one involving much maneuvering between the White House, the various Congressional factions, and representatives of the railroads themselves.[20] At first some attempt was made by President Taft to unite Republicans from both wings of the party behind an administration bill. Cummins and Clapp were invited to attend a White House conference on the subject before Congress met in December 1909 along with cabinet members and conservatives such as Elihu Root.[21] But the insurgents were suspicious of these proceedings even before they had begun, believing that the conservatives would be allowed to frame the bill. Cummins was doubtful whether he ought to go to Washington at all before Congress opened, and other progressive Republican Senators advised him not to commit himself to any proposal until they had all had a chance to go over it together.[22] They must have been even more suspicious

[18] Bristow to Prof. H. J. Hoover, March 7, 1910, *ibid.*

[19] Hechler, *Insurgency,* pp. 158–162.

[20] *Ibid.,* pp. 163–177; Mowry, *Theodore Roosevelt and the Progressive Movement,* pp. 94–103.

[21] New York *Times,* Nov. 9, 1909; Senator Moses E. Clapp to Bristow, Oct. 23, 1909, Bristow Papers.

[22] Cummins to Bristow, Sept. 22, 1909, Bristow Papers; Bristow to Cummins, Oct. 30, 1909, *ibid.*; Bristow to Clapp, Oct. 30, 1909, *ibid.*; Clapp to Bristow, Oct. 23, 1909, *ibid.*

about the forthcoming bill when the press reported the presence of prominent railroad presidents at White House conferences.

When the administration bill eventually arrived in Congress, the insurgents gave it a hostile reception. In the House they combined with the Democrats again to strike out sections of the bill declaring the Sherman Anti-trust Act to be inoperative in certain types of railroad mergers, added sections providing for the physical evaluation of railroad assets and for long-and-short-haul regulation, and made telephone and telegraph companies subject to regulation by defining them as common carriers. In the Senate the progressive Republicans threatened to append equally drastic amendments, and Aldrich was able to save the situation only by striking a bargain with the Democrats whereby some of their votes were traded for Aldrich's support on another unrelated issue. Though some of the ground gained in the House was thereby lost in the Senate, the insurgents had succeeded in making some important changes in the legislation — enough to persuade them to vote for it on the final roll call.[23]

Between this militant determination of the insurgents to press ahead with progressive reform on the one hand and the uncompromising response of the standpat leadership on the other, the Republican party split wide open in 1910. During the Roosevelt years Jonathan Dolliver of Iowa had been a regular Republican Senator with mild tendencies toward insurgency. By the late summer of 1909 he was not merely miffed with the party leadership in Congress but ready to set out on a crusade to destroy it. Learning of the President's praise of Aldrich as "the real leader of the Senate," he wrote to Beveridge, " 'Leader of the Senate' — we will jar that myth in the next three years. . . . We will all go in with the common weapons of truth and good sense and make a new era in national life." [24] About the same time conservative Republicans in Iowa were organizing to drive men like Dolliver out of the

[23] New York *Times,* May 11, 1910; *ibid.,* June 4, 1910; *ibid.,* June 15, 1910.
[24] Dolliver to Beveridge, Sept. 14, 1909, Beveridge Papers.

party. An uncompromising policy "may not bring office or party honors," one of them wrote, "but it will bear good fruit in the struggle that must be fought out, before we eliminate populistic principles with Cummins, La Follette and Kendall from the Republican party." [25]

If there was any possibility of renewed Republican unity after the great Congressional battles of 1909 and 1910, it lay in the hands of President Taft. For though the insurgents grew increasingly distrustful of the President as his term progressed, their attacks were at first directed at Cannon and Aldrich rather than the administration. In the first two years of his administration they were noticeably reluctant to break openly with Taft, whose nomination and election they had ardently supported in 1908. It was one thing to assail Aldrich, the Senator from Rhode Island, or Cannon, the Congressman from Danville, Illinois, but altogether a more serious matter for politicians as partisan as the insurgents to attack a President of their own party. Had he chosen, Taft might have capitalized on the progressives' disinclination to challenge the administration. Though the insurgent revolt placed him in an awkward position, he could have stayed aloof, to some extent, from the congressional squabbles. He might have attempted to make the presidency a source of Republican unity, concentrating on policies that would bring Republicans together and striving to find compromises where they disagreed.

Instead, Taft completely alienated the insurgents during his first two years in office and practically forced them into open opposition to his administration. Rather than attempting to act as a balance wheel between the Republican factions in Congress, the President sided with the Old Guard at every important crisis. Though he had come into office with a plan of his own to unseat Speaker Cannon, he threw his influence against the House insurgents when they made their bid in March 1909. Despite his original commitment to downward revision of the tariff, he came to be a close ally of Aldrich and

---

[25] Ellsworth Rominger to John F. Lacey, Feb. 12, 1910, Lacey Papers. Kendall was a progressive Republican Congressman from Iowa.

to believe that the Payne-Aldrich bill was the best tariff measure ever passed. And though he favored effective railroad regulation and a postal savings bank system, he managed to quarrel with the insurgents on these issues too.[26]

These legislative tangles were, of course, by no means easy
matters for the President to handle. It would have been very
difficult and perhaps impossible for him to have avoided alienating one side or the other. And if he had been forced to
choose between the insurgent and regular factions in Congress, it was only logical for him to side with the regulars,
since they were by far the larger group. "When . . . certain
Republicans decline to go into the caucus, and stand out 30
to 190, it would be the sacrifice of every interest I represent
to side with the insurgents, however much sympathy I may
feel with the principles in respect to the House rules that they
seek to carry out," Taft argued at the beginning of his administration.[27]

But Taft did not merely offend the insurgents by failing to
support them on legislative matters. It was as much his public
statements and executive policies that upset them, and these
cannot be attributed to the exigencies of Congressional politics. Though it might have been inevitable that the President
bow to Aldrich on the tariff schedules, there was absolutely
no need for him to defend the Payne-Aldrich tariff as the best
ever passed, as he did in September 1909 at Winona, Minnesota, in the heart of progressive Republican territory. The
tariff insurgents took this speech, together with his praise of
Aldrich in Boston a few days before, as a gratuitous insult to
them and their well-known efforts to revise the tariff. Nor did
Taft's handling of the famous Pinchot-Ballinger dispute,
which convinced most progressives that the administration
had turned against Roosevelt's conservation policies, have anything to do with legislative maneuvering. Finally by cutting
off the insurgents' patronage and throwing the influence of
the administration against them in the primary elections of

[26] Mowry, *Era of Theodore Roosevelt,* pp. 239–246, 260–262.
[27] William Howard Taft to William Allen White, March 12, 1909,
White Papers.

1910, Taft virtually declared war on the progressive wing of the party.[28]

In view of all this, it is remarkable how long most of the progressive Republicans withheld direct personal criticism of President Taft. When the Pinchot-Ballinger dispute first became public late in 1909, Pinchot was quick to deny that he was opposed to the policies of the President.[29] After the Winona speech Cummins wrote that though he and Dolliver would not shrink from the President's challenge, he did not intend "to make personal war upon the President." [30] Though they were highly critical of the administration's railroad bill in 1910, insurgent orators in Congress were careful not to make personal references to Taft himself.[31] Opening the Iowa election campaign in May 1910, Cummins and Dolliver attacked Aldrich, Cannon, Attorney General Wickersham, and the Iowa standpatters, but again made no direct reference to the President.[32] By July, Cummins was saying in private that Taft's "unwarrantable interference in the Iowa campaign" had made him feel "a little more belligerent," but the furthest he was prepared to move publicly against Taft was to urge the state convention to withhold its customary blanket endorsement of the national administration.[33] Dolliver's last great Senate speech came closest to being an open, direct attack on the President before the midterm elections, and it was not delivered till June 13, nine months after Taft's Winona speech.

Privately, however, progressive Republican opinion was extremely hostile to Taft well before this time. Joseph Bristow's letters mirror the slow but steady insurgent disillusionment with the President, which began soon after he assumed office. Less than a month after Taft's inauguration, Bristow remarked that nearly all of the progressives felt the President's

---

[28] Mowry, *Era of Theodore Roosevelt,* pp. 266–267.

[29] New York *Times,* August 13, 1909.

[30] Cummins to Bristow, Sept. 22, 1909, Bristow Papers.

[31] New York *Times,* April 26, 1910.

[32] *Ibid.,* May 11, 1910.

[33] Cummins to Dolliver, July 6, 1910, Dolliver Papers; Cummins to Bristow, July 7, 1910, Bristow Papers.

opinion to be against them on every proposition, though personally Bristow found Taft talking "just like he always has. He seems to be interested in the genuine tariff revision and in favor of the progressive ideas." [34] In May 1909, he was reporting confidentially that the insurgents were receiving no support from the White House on the tariff and expressing surprise that Taft should not be aiding their fight for revision downward.[35] By June Bristow noted a general impression that Taft "is with the Aldrich crowd" but added, "I don't think he is at heart." [36] On August 11 Bristow still thought that "President Taft's heart was with us in our fight," but by the end of the month he was saying that while "Cummins has some hope that he will yet right about and stand for the right things . . . I have about given up." [37] Bristow was still willing to give Taft the benefit of the doubt as late as December 1909. "The President wants some good things done," he wrote. "The danger is that he will yield." [38] But soon there was an abrupt change in tone. "He is a great fellow to talk," Bristow wrote bitterly of Taft in January 1910. "We found that out during the tariff fight, but when the critical test comes, Mr. Aldrich inserts into the bill what he wants and Taft alleges that it is the very thing." [39] By February Bristow believed Taft was "as much a reactionary as Aldrich in his heart," [40] and by April, not even entitled to pity. "If he is so ignorant and indolent as not to know or realize what is going on in his administration—that Ballinger is the friend of crooks, that Wickersham is the envoy of Wall St., that Dickinson is the envoy of the Harriman interests, and Knox is the minister of the Steel trust and the Pennsylvania railroad, that Nagel is emissary of the Standard Oil Company and the brewers, it seems

[34] Bristow to Fred W. Trigg, April 7, 1909, Bristow Papers.

[35] Bristow to Harold T. Chase, May 23, 1909, *ibid.*

[36] Bristow to William Allen White, June 8, 1909, *ibid.*

[37] Bristow to A. A. Graham, August 11, 1909, *ibid.*; Bristow to Col. Nelson, August 30, 1909, *ibid.*

[38] Bristow to Fred S. Jackson, Dec. 6, 1909, *ibid.*

[39] Bristow to William Allen White, Jan. 19, 1910, *ibid.*

[40] Bristow to Harold T. Chase, Feb. 12, 1910, *ibid.*

to me he is more an object of contempt than pity. If he does not know the characteristics of these men, then he is the worst man that has been at the head of the American government since Martin Van Buren." [41]

Other progressive Republicans took longer to come to such conclusions, some lost hope in Taft sooner than Bristow, but the general trend of insurgent opinion was toward steadily increasing hostility to the President. For many of them, especially the Senators, it was Taft's speech in praise of the Payne-Aldrich tariff at Winona that finally made it clear that they could expect no aid from the White House. "Up to that time," Cummins wrote privately, "I held fast to my faith in his [Taft's] sympathy with the progressive policies that the country demands; but when I read that speech in connection with what he said at Boston,[42] it seems clear to me that he intends to take Aldrich for the leader, and that we might as well get ready to make our fight without him." [43] Senator Clapp saw no point in the insurgents attending White House conferences on legislation after this. "You know as well as I do," he wrote to Bristow, "that there is no likelihood that we can ever stand for any legislation which they will frame, nor would they stand for any legislation which we would frame." [44] Bristow and Cummins were no more sanguine about the outcome of such conferences.[45]

Thus, despite their reluctance to break openly and completely with the administration, the progressive Republicans had given up all hope of working with Taft before the midterm elections of 1910. And when the results of the summer primaries and the November elections became known, the insurgents were ready to begin moving openly against the ad-

---

[41] Bristow to Chase, April 11, 1911, *ibid.*

[42] It was in a speech at Boston where Taft referred to Aldrich as the "real leader of the Senate."

[43] Cummins to Bristow, Sept. 22, 1909, Bristow Papers.

[44] Clapp to Bristow, Oct. 23, 1909, *ibid.*

[45] Bristow to Clapp, Oct. 30, 1909, *ibid.*; Bristow to Cummins, Oct. 30, 1909, *ibid.*; Cummins to Beveridge, Oct. 1, 1909, Beveridge Papers.

ministration. The returns seemed to indicate both a massive public repudiation of Taft and the conservative Republicans, and a vote of confidence in the insurgents. In the primary elections of 1910, 41 incumbent Republican Congressmen were overthrown, almost every one of them standpatters.[46] On the other hand the insurgents maintained and improved their position, especially in the progressive strongholds of the west. In Wisconsin La Follette and the insurgent Congressmen were renominated, while the single standpat Representative from that state was defeated by a progressive.[47] The large insurgent delegation from Minnesota also remained intact, and a progressive candidate defeated Congressman Tawney, the only Minnesota Congressman to vote for the Payne-Aldrich tariff bill.[48] In Iowa the progressive forces won control of the state Republican convention and refused to endorse the Taft administration. Every insurgent Congressman was renominated, and Colonel J. A. T. Hull, a standpatter who had represented his Congressional district for many years, was defeated by a progressive challenger.[49] The Kansas progressives defeated four standpat Congressmen, increasing the size of the insurgent delegation from Kansas to six.[50] Two House insurgents, Asle J. Gronna and Miles Poindexter, won Senate seats in North Dakota and Washington respectively, and Hiram Johnson led a progressive Republican ticket to a sweeping primary victory in California.[51]

The conservative Republicans were dealt another blow in the general elections when the Democrats scored landslide victories all over the country. Nearly all of the Democratic gains were made at the expense of conservative rather than insurgent

[46] Mowry, *Theodore Roosevelt and the Progressive Movement,* p. 130.
[47] New York *Times,* Sept. 7, 1910.
[48] New York *Times,* Nov. 9, 1910.
[49] Mowry, *Theodore Roosevelt and the Progressive Movement,* pp. 115, 128.
[50] New York *Times,* August 3, 1910.
[51] *Ibid.,* August 18, 1910; *ibid.,* Sept. 15, 1910; Phillips, *Gronna,* p. 299.

Republicans.[52] Of the 59 seats which the Democrats gained in the House, for instance, only two were won in progressive Republican states. On the other hand the Democrats won twelve House seats in New York, eight in Ohio, five in Illinois, and four in Pennsylvania, Missouri, New Jersey, and West Virginia. The insurgents were understandably jubilant at these results. While the Republicans had done well in the progressive states, Bristow pointed out, they had fared badly wherever standpatters were in control.[53] From this he drew the conclusion that a great future awaited the progressive Republican movement.

They might have paused in their self-congratulation had they looked a little more closely at the election returns from Indiana, where the progressive Republicans suffered their only important loss in 1910 — the defeat of Senator Albert J. Beveridge by a Democrat. During the campaign several of the insurgent Senators came to the aid of Beveridge in his bid for re-election; and as practical politicians they acknowledged that a different kind of campaign was necessary in this state, because unlike the usual progressive Republican state, Indiana had a well developed two-party system.[54] In Indiana the progressive Republicans deemed it unwise to attack the Republican Old Guard as freely as they were wont to do further west or to play up the difference between wings of the party, for anti-Republican sentiment was expected to benefit the Democrats.[55] Beveridge himself had taken care to stay closer to the administration than the other insurgents. "Let us have no row with the President unless it really exists; and let us hope and pray that there will be no occasion for any row with him," Beveridge admonished a friendly editor who had published stories implying antagonism between Taft and Beveridge.[56] Intraparty battles just did not pay dividends in a two-party state like Indiana as they did in states like Iowa or Kansas

[52] New York *Times,* Nov. 9 and 10, 1910.
[53] Bristow to Robert P. Bass, Nov. 10, 1910, Bristow Papers.
[54] Bristow to Beveridge, August 27, 1910, *ibid.*
[55] Cummins to Beveridge, Sept. 6, 1910, Beveridge Papers.
[56] Beveridge to Rudolph G. Leeds, March 10, 1910, *ibid.*

where the Democrats were hardly ever a serious threat to Republican hegemony.

While the 1910 elections confirmed the solid grip progressive Republicans held over certain western and midwestern states, the overall results had ominous implications for the movement. The insurgents could only further the cause of progressivism within the Republican party by attacking its conservative leadership, but a national reaction against this leadership benefited mainly the Democrats. Early in 1910 Joseph Bristow remarked hopefully, "The country doesn't want to go Democratic. It wants to stay Republican." Then as an afterthought he added, "Kansas wants to stay with the Republican party. In my judgement so does Iowa." [57] The insurgents were to find that what was true in Iowa and Kansas was not necessarily true in the nation at large.

---

[57] Bristow to F. S. Jackson, Jan. 11, 1910, Bristow Papers.

# chapter four

# The Bid for National Power

After the crushing Republican defeats in the midterm elections of 1910, it was widely speculated that a "harmony" movement was about to develop in the party. In December President Taft invited a number of leading insurgent Senators to the White House for conferences over patronage, and all but La Follette accepted the invitations.[1] This development dismayed some irreconcilable standpatters; one Iowan suggested that if the President showed any further signs of weakness they might be forced to shift their support to Vice-President Sherman or some other reliable man for 1912.[2] Taft also seemed to be making a gesture toward harmony through some of his appointments in 1911, especially that of Henry L. Stimson, a Roosevelt associate, as Secretary of War.[3]

In Congress too, there were indications of easier relationships between conservative and progressive Republicans. On December 13, 1910, Sereno Payne, chairman of the House Ways and Means committee, announced that he favored a schedule-by-schedule revision of the tariff and predicted the passage at the coming session of a bill to create a permanent tariff commission, a proposal favored by the progressive wing of the party.[4] In the Senate on the same day, the Finance

---

[1] New York *Times,* Dec. 4, 1910; *ibid.,* Dec. 7, 1910.

[2] John F. Lacey to Frank D. Jackson, Dec. 8, 1910, Lacey Papers.

[3] New York *Times,* May 13, 1911.

[4] *Ibid.,* Dec. 14, 1910.

committee authorized the appointment of a subcommittee to draft a bill creating a tariff commission; and the conservative leader Henry Cabot Lodge gave his support to a resolution moved by Cummins that was designed to open the way for revision by schedule. When the special session of the Sixty-second Congress convened in April 1911, the new Republican floor leader in the House, James R. Mann, directly reversed the policy followed by Cannon in the previous sessions by awarding favorable committee assignments to insurgent Congressmen.[5]

Further rapprochement between the divided Republican factions in Congress seemed possible as a result of the strange new alignments which arose from the issue of the Canadian reciprocity treaty. This was an agreement negotiated with the Canadian government by the Secretary of State, providing for a reciprocal lowering of tariff rates between Canada and the United States. Nearly all the Republicans in the Senate were opposed to this Taft proposal, Knute Nelson reported, but some did not want to vote against the President.[6] When the treaty came to a final vote in the Senate, twelve Republican insurgents were joined by twelve Republican regulars against the measure, while three insurgents and eighteen regulars

---

[5] *Ibid.*, April 12, 1911.
[6] Knute Nelson to Ole C. Canestorp, March 9, 1911, Knute Nelson Papers, Minnesota Historical Society, St. Paul, Minnesota.

voted for it.[7] In the House Cannon and Norris found themselves voting alongside each other. From this breakdown of
the lines established in the previous Congress, there might con-
ceivably have come generally improved relationships between
the two wings of the Republican party.

But by 1911 the insurgents had lost all faith in the President and the conservative wing of the party, and some were
already laying plans to oppose Taft's renomination in 1912.[8]
"I do not think there is much possibility of this alleged harmony that is being so much discussed," Bristow wrote in December 1910. "We are going to fight for the right kind of legislation, just as we have, and the reactionaries will still have
influence with Taft." [9] Any report that the insurgents were
being treated equally by the administration in regards to patronage, Norris wrote in January 1911, "is untrue, and is made
only for the purpose of enlisting public sentiment." [10]

In Congress the conservative-progressive split in the Republican party soon proved to be as deep as ever, despite the few
earlier indications to the contrary. At the opening of the special session of Congress in April 1911, forty-one Congressmen
and ten Senators held their own insurgent Republican caucuses and presented a number of demands to the regular organizations. The Senators asked for one quarter of the majority committee places on the grounds that this would fairly
reflect the composition of the Republican party in the Senate
—38 regulars and 13 insurgents.[11] They even demanded that
the four insurgents on the committee on committees be given
the task of allocating this progressive representation. But the
regulars refused to accept these proposals, arguing with good
reason that the insurgents were establishing themselves as a
separate party in the Senate.[12] The Republican leadership

---

[7] New York *Times,* July 23, 1911.
[8] Gifford Pinchot to William Allen White, Dec. 5, 1910, White Papers.
[9] Bristow to Frank B. Bristow, Dec. 10, 1910, Bristow Papers.
[10] Norris to John E. Arnold, Jan. 19, 1911, Norris Papers.
[11] New York *Times,* April 4, 1911.
[12] *Ibid.,* April 22, 1911.

then further alienated the progressives by denying La Follette a place on the Interstate Commerce committee.[13]

Thus, the Sixty-second Congress began with a reassertion of insurgent solidarity and Republican division despite the efforts of House leader Mann and others to promote harmony. What is more, although the regular-insurgent division disappeared temporarily during the debates on reciprocity, it reappeared later in the Congress when the Democratic-insurgent coalition was revived to pass the so-called "pop-gun" tariff bills, single schedule reductions of the tariff rates, which Taft vetoed.[14]

By 1911, however, the center of political interest was shifting from Congress to the White House as a presidential election approached. For the next two years, Republican party divisions would turn more on the question of who was to be the presidential nominee in 1912 than on any issue before the Congress. It was precisely at this point that Taft, by injecting the reciprocity issue into national politics, produced the kind of direct confrontation between himself and the insurgents that he had largely avoided in 1909 and 1910 when Cannon and Aldrich were the main targets of progressive wrath. By this time it would have required herculean efforts for Taft to win back the confidence of the insurgents. Typically Taft chose instead to take up an issue which drove them further into opposition.

It was only to be expected that as the insurgents grew increasingly disenchanted with Taft they should begin considering the possibility of returning Theodore Roosevelt to the White House. Memories of his administration could only grow sweeter as they compared their experiences under him with those under his successor. As early as September 1909 Jonathan Dolliver had written to Albert Beveridge, "With Pinchot knocked out and Aldrich put in command, I think you can hear a lion roar in East Africa," obliquely referring to the

---

[13] *Ibid.,* April 27, 1911.
[14] Mowry, *Theodore Roosevelt and the Progressive Movement,* p. 167.

itinerant Roosevelt.[15] At a dinner given in New York City in January 1910, Henry J. Allen, a progressive editor from Kansas and a former law partner of Senator Bristow, declared that Taft would not be able to carry a single township in Kansas, and he called upon Roosevelt to save the party from defeat.[16] Even Robert La Follette, never an unqualified admirer of Roosevelt's, was moved to declare in 1910 that the ex-President was the greatest living American.[17]

But in the early months of 1911 when the insurgents were organizing to oppose Taft's renomination at the 1912 convention, Roosevelt was unwilling to enter the race for the presidency. He believed that Taft, through his control of the party machinery, was bound to win renomination; after that the Democrats would certainly win the election. The best strategy, Roosevelt counseled at this stage, was to accept this course of events as inevitable, and then to set about reorganizing the Republican party for 1916. Roosevelt did not think anyone should challenge Taft for the nomination, and he certainly did not intend doing so himself.[18]

The insurgents could not accept this course of action with equanimity. The unpopularity of Taft seemed to present the progressives with a golden opportunity to win the nomination for one of their own number, and the prospect of running for office in 1912 on a ticket headed by such a disastrously weak candidate as Taft appalled them. William Allen White wrote in May 1911 that he had "yet to find the first man who really believes that Kansas will go Republican if Taft is nominated." What is more, if the Democrats nominated Woodrow Wilson on a progressive platform, White predicted that "the Republican party in the Mississippi Valley and the mountain states along the Pacific coast would be wiped off the map, and only such states as by their platforms repudiated the national plat-

---

[15] Dolliver to Beveridge, Sept. 14, 1909, Dolliver Papers.
[16] New York *Times*, Jan. 30, 1910.
[17] *Ibid.*, June 28, 1910.
[18] Mowry, *Theodore Roosevelt and the Progressive Movement*, p. 176.

form would be able to save themselves from ruin." [19] A progressive candidacy for the Republican nomination, even one doomed to failure, might at least save the progressive Republican movement in the midwest from collapse by enabling the insurgents to disassociate themselves from Taft. The chances were all in favor of the President's renomination, Norris admitted, "but it will pay to make the fight anyway." [20] Bristow warned that "if we acquiesce in this Taft movement and make no fight, we are stamped with the Taft brand which puts us in the minority in Kansas." [21]

With Roosevelt refusing to commit himself, who was to be the progressives' candidate? Gifford Pinchot, writing to White in December 1910, thought that in view of Roosevelt's emphatic refusal to enter the race, Senators La Follette and Cummins were the only possibilities.[22] White replied that La Follette, Cummins, or Beveridge would all be acceptable candidates.[23] But Beveridge was out of office by 1911, and Cummins was unwilling to commit himself at this point, despite La Follette's offer of support.[24] Consequently, at a series of conferences held in Washington in the early months of 1911, most of the insurgents agreed to support the candidacy of La Follette, as the strongest man they could put in the field.[25]

A somewhat disguised La Follette organization had already been established in January 1911 in the form of a National Progressive Republican League. The President of this organization was Senator Bourne of Oregon; many other prominent progressive Republicans such as George Norris, Gifford Pin-

---

[19] William Allen White to Fred C. Trigg, May 27, 1911, White Papers.
[20] Norris to Ray McCarl, July 10, 1911, Norris Papers.
[21] Bristow to Harold T. Chase, August 9, 1911, Bristow Papers.
[22] Pinchot to White, Dec. 5, 1910, White Papers.
[23] White to Gifford Pinchot, Dec. 8, 1910, White Papers.
[24] New York *Times*, April 11, 1912; La Follette, *Autobiography*, pp. 220–222; Norris to John O. Yeiser, Jan. 27, 1912, Norris Papers.
[25] Norris to William B. Ely, May 23, 1911, Norris Papers; Norris to John O. Yeiser, *ibid.*

chot, and Senators Bristow and Clapp were charter members.[26] Its declared purpose was the publicizing of progressive principles rather than the support of a presidential candidacy, but it was generally interpreted by both friend and foe as a vehicle for La Follette's presidential campaign.[27] Through the early months of 1911 La Follette worked on the organization of his campaign, and when by June he was assured of sufficient political and financial support, he made a public announcement of his candidacy.[28]

At no stage did La Follette's presidential campaign develop real national strength. Even La Follette's warmest friends and supporters such as Joseph Bristow admitted that the Wisconsin Senator had little chance of winning the nomination.[29] "Bourne is the only man who is optimistic about his chances," Albert Cummins reported in July, "and his faith is founded rather upon a revolution yet to come than upon existing facts." [30] The progressives blamed this weakness on the President's control of the party machinery, certainly the main obstacle before any Republican hopeful. But few political observers, whether progressive or conservative, doubted that Roosevelt had a much greater chance of winning the nomination, if he should choose to enter the race, though he would face the same difficulty.

It soon became apparent that La Follette's support was confined largely to the hard-core insurgent Republican states of the agrarian midwest. Moderate eastern progressives declined to support La Follette on the grounds that he was generally distrusted in their section of the country.[31] The businessmen of the country feared La Follette, a Washington newspaper correspondent reported, "and this is particularly true of the

[26] New York *Times,* Jan. 24, 1911; La Follette to William Allen White, Dec. 28, 1910, White Papers.

[27] White to La Follette, Jan. 3, 1911, *ibid.*; Mowry, *Theodore Roosevelt and the Progressive Movement,* p. 172.

[28] La Follette, *Autobiography,* p. 224.

[29] Bristow to Harold T. Chase, August 9, 1911, Bristow Papers.

[30] Cummins to Beveridge, July 3, 1911, Beveridge Papers.

[31] Henry L. Stimson to Gifford Pinchot, Feb. 25, 1911, Gifford Pinchot Papers, Library of Congress.

east." [32] Measured by "delegate-getting standards," the editor Mark Sullivan explained in December 1911 to a Minnesota progressive, "La Follette has never made the faintest impression, practically, east of the Ohio." Sullivan doubted whether La Follette had ever made a speech in New York City.[33] Nor was La Follette strong in the more easterly, urbanized states of the midwest. There was little La Follette sentiment in Michigan, a progressive Republican reported in December 1911, and the same was true of Ohio.[34] At a conference of western Governors held in Cleveland at this time, James R. Garfield was surprised to find that "La Follette sentiment is not as strong as I had supposed." He wrote to Gifford Pinchot that the feeling was that La Follette could not overcome the "unfair prejudice that exists in the minds of so many people against him," a prejudice "not confined to the men that you and I ordinarily meet," but existing as well "among some of the strong labor leaders and farmers." [35] The people "have put La Follette down as an agitator," Henry Allen of Kansas lamented. "His Frenchy name has its effect in causing people to immediately jump at the conclusion that his temperament is French and that he is the last word in the book of 'Radicalism.' " [36]

Though most of this antipathy to La Follette was couched in terms of personal distaste for the Senator from Wisconsin, the weakness of his candidacy surely reflected the limited influence of the insurgent movement in the Republican party at its height. For the insurgents had agreed early in 1911 that La Follette was the strongest candidate they could field against Taft, and his weaknesses were their weaknesses also, the "Frenchy name" excepted. None of the other insurgents was

---

[32] J. C. O'Laughlin to Theodore Roosevelt, Dec. 10, 1911, Roosevelt Papers.

[33] Mark Sullivan to George S. Loftus, Dec. 27, 1911, James Manahan Papers, Minnesota Historical Society, St. Paul, Minnesota.

[34] Frank Knox to Roosevelt, Dec. 6, 1911, Roosevelt Papers; James R. Garfield to Roosevelt, Nov. 21, 1911, *ibid.*; New York *Times,* Nov. 21, 1911.

[35] Garfield to Gifford Pinchot, Dec. 2, 1911, Pinchot Papers.

[36] Henry J. Allen to Bristow, Jan. 6, 1912, Bristow Papers.

well known east of the Ohio, few of them had given a speech in New York City, and they were collectively referred to by the national press as "the radical faction" of the Republican party.

By contrast Theodore Roosevelt had tremendous political strength throughout the country in 1911. This popular support for Roosevelt among rank-and-file Republicans, culminating in his sweeping victories in the 1912 presidential primaries, has been taken as evidence that the average Republican voter was a "progressive" by 1912.[37] No doubt there is a measure of truth in this interpretation, but the attractiveness of Theodore Roosevelt to the progressive Republican politicians in 1911 lay precisely in the fact that a Roosevelt candidacy was expected to appeal to a far wider spectrum of American opinion than the Cummins–La Follette style of progressivism.

Whether or not Roosevelt was really a progressive was debated in the Taft years as it has been in more recent historical literature, and it was recognized at the time that Roosevelt's progressivism, if such it was, differed considerably from La Follette's. His views on the question of industrial combination, for instance, placed him in direct opposition to most of the insurgents on the single most important issue of the day. But it was generally more superficial considerations that made Roosevelt seem less radical, and consequently more appealing a candidate than La Follette in 1911. He had, for instance, taken no public position on the Payne-Aldrich tariff and had campaigned for conservative Republicans such as Henry Cabot Lodge in the elections of 1910. Many Republican politicians who were not noted for advanced progressive views turned to Roosevelt in 1912 as the only man who could appeal to both wings of the party in 1912.[38]

Linked with this view of Roosevelt as a man of more moderate views than La Follette was a wholly nonideological fac-

---

[37] Mowry, *Theodore Roosevelt and the Progressive Movement*, p. 236.

[38] L. B. Hanna (Congressman–North Dakota) to Roosevelt, Dec. 11, 1911, Roosevelt Papers.

tor—the tremendous appeal of the Roosevelt personality to the public at large. After the 1912 elections William Allen White estimated that Roosevelt's Progressive party had benefited by perhaps a million "Teddy-votes — votes of men," he explained to Roosevelt, "who had confidence in you personally, without any particular intelligent reason to give why; except that you were a masculine sort of person with extremely masculine virtues and palpably masculine faults." [39] In another letter to Roosevelt, Senator Borah wrote of a cross-continental rail trip he made in the summer of 1910. "Every man, woman, and child whom I met on the train or elsewhere who knew or ascertained that I was lately from Washington would invariably say without a moment's hesitation, 'Well, how is Roosevelt? How is Teddy?' These questions came as naturally as one would ask about a close personal friend. I never expect to see, Colonel Roosevelt, such a universal feeling of devotion to a man as the good common people of this country exhibit towards you." [40] Without the help of Roosevelt, the progressive Republicans would have remained a small minority group within their party, strong only in one underpopulated region of the country, and without any hope of achieving national power. But by attaching themselves to Roosevelt's unique political magnetism, they were able to transform themselves into a force to be reckoned with in national politics.

The switch from La Follette to Roosevelt that occurred during the latter months of 1911 and the early part of 1912 was not accomplished without a certain amount of soul-searching on the part of the progressive Republicans. Some men like Gifford Pinchot and Medill McCormick, two of the villains of La Follette's *Autobiography,* had little compunction about abandoning La Follette for Roosevelt except for the personal embarrassment involved. But western insurgents like Bristow and Norris were aware that the move from La Follette to Roosevelt had more than personal implications. Few of them went so far as La Follette himself, who denounced Roosevelt as a

---

[39] White to Roosevelt, Sept. 24, 1913, White Papers.
[40] William E. Borah to Roosevelt, July 9, 1910, Roosevelt Papers.

complete fake, but they were dimly aware that the ex-President did not stand for quite the same things as they did. With considerable justice, Bristow grumbled that Roosevelt's scheme for federal incorporation of the trusts "is what the trusts all want." [41] Others complained of his silence on the tariff issue, of his actions as President in the Tennessee Iron and Steel Company merger case, and of his cooperation with the Republican Old Guard in earlier days.[42]

Usually Roosevelt's progressive critics did not credit him with having genuinely different political views of his own but saw him as a "side-stepper and a dodger," a man who knew what was right but who had a weakness for compromise.[43] They cited his behavior in the elections of 1910, when instead of siding with the insurgents in their battle against the Old Guard, Roosevelt had tried to hold the party together by campaigning for an assortment of moderate progressives and outright conservatives. Unlike La Follette, Bristow commented, who had "fought along a consistent, well-thought-out plan," Roosevelt had "plunged here and there as impulse has indicated. Roosevelt has a spectacular manner. He is the greatest advertiser that has appeared in modern times, and catches the popular fancy; but he has not that well-grounded, deep-seated, well-matured plan and conviction along the lines of economic reform that Mr. La Follette has. And he is a compromiser in a crisis." [44] So suspicious were some insurgents of the Roosevelt boom in its early stages that they put it down as a reactionary scheme to divide and defeat the progressive forces.[45]

But despite these doubts, all the prominent insurgents were eventually drawn into the Roosevelt camp, the embittered La

[41] Bristow to White, Jan. 11, 1912, Bristow Papers.
[42] Ole Hanson to Miles Poindexter, March 20, 1912, Poindexter Papers; Harry N. Jones to White, July 18, 1912, White Papers; R. R. Rees to White, May 2, 1912, *ibid.*
[43] Bristow to White, Jan. 19, 1912, White Papers; White to Bristow, Dec. 28, 1911, *ibid.*
[44] Bristow to Henry J. Allen, Dec. 29, 1911, Bristow Papers.
[45] Norris to F. P. Corrick, Dec. 19, 1911, Norris Papers; Bristow to White, Dec. 20, 1911, Bristow Papers.

Follette excepted. Though he still preferred La Follette, Bristow wrote in April 1912, it had become increasingly clear to him that "the only man that could make effective headway against Taft in the central and eastern part of the country was Mr. Roosevelt. While we could have carried a part of the western states with Mr. La Follette he could not have secured under any circumstances . . . more than one third of the convention."[46] Norris wrote that "no man was more enthusiastic in his support of La Follette than I was, and yet, . . . I could not close my eyes to the fact that in the present contest the people seemed to want Roosevelt."[47] It was conceded in every quarter that in a battle between Taft and La Follette, Taft would certainly be nominated. Only Roosevelt could head off this catastrophe.[48] And so, on the grounds of expediency, the insurgents turned to Roosevelt's leadership for the 1912 campaign.

When it first became apparent that Roosevelt was edging his way into the presidential race, some progressive Republicans feared a division of progressive strength between Roosevelt and La Follette that would enable Taft to win many convention delegates he would otherwise have lost. Norris warned of this danger in Nebraska and urged Roosevelt to take himself out of the contest in that state. In Nebraska itself, Norris advised his supporters to stick to La Follette but to avoid an open fight with the Roosevelt forces at all cost.[49] Elsewhere progressives tried to organize progressive delegations free to support either La Follette or Roosevelt at the national convention.[50] The progressive Republican organization in South Dakota included the names of both La Follette and Roosevelt in its letterhead, just to be on the safe side.

---

[46] Bristow to W. H. Olin, April 30, 1912, *ibid.*
[47] Norris to M. E. Wells, Feb. 29, 1912, Norris Papers.
[48] Hiram Johnson to Roosevelt, Oct. 20, 1911, Roosevelt Papers; W. R. Stubbs to Roosevelt, Dec. 4, 1911, *ibid.*; New York *Times*, Feb. 26, 1912; Miles Poindexter to Samuel Archer, May 11, 1912, Poindexter Papers; White to Bristow, Dec. 28, 1911, White Papers.
[49] Norris to F. P. Corrick, Jan. 4, 1912, Norris Papers.
[50] Bristow to Geo. W. Hanna, Feb. 1, 1912, Bristow Papers.

Later, when it had become clear that the Roosevelt movement was developing far more strength than the La Follette campaign, the fear arose that La Follette's refusal to accept Roosevelt as the progressive standard-bearer would weaken the movement to upset Taft. In South Dakota Senator Crawford was warned by a number of progressives that the state would go to Taft unless La Follette ceased his attacks on Roosevelt.[51] Men like Bristow and Norris who had remained in the La Follette camp until his candidacy was obviously beyond hope of success were outraged by La Follette's behavior.[52] But by the early months of 1912 the tide was running toward Roosevelt so fast that the sole effect of La Follette's broadsides was to leave him a completely isolated figure in the progressive Republican movement for several years.

Roosevelt had not changed his mind about entering the presidential campaign until near the end of 1911.[53] But once he had decided to make the race after all, his candidacy developed remarkable strength in a very short time. In February 1912 Roosevelt made his famous announcement that his hat was in the ring, and in the next few months he went on to win a series of smashing victories in the Republican presidential primaries, defeating Taft not only in progressive strongholds like California and Minnesota, but also in eastern and industrial states like Pennsylvania, Illinois, and Ohio.[54] In the end, however, Roosevelt's earlier forecasts proved to be cor-

---

[51] R. D. Venney to Coe L. Crawford, March 22, 1912, Coe L. Crawford Papers, South Dakota State Historical Society, Pierre, South Dakota; Thomas Thorson to Crawford, March 28, 1912, *ibid.*; E. L. Senn to Crawford, March 28, 1912, *ibid.*; John Sutherland to Crawford, Feb. 13, 1912, *ibid.*; Charles E. Deland to Crawford, March 19, 1912, *ibid.*

[52] Bristow to R. A. Harris, March 20, 1912, Bristow Papers; Norris to J. J. McCarthy, March 25, 1912, Norris Papers.

[53] Mowry, *Theodore Roosevelt and the Progressive Movement,* pp. 187–196.

[54] New York *Times,* April 10, 1912 (Illinois); April 14, 1912 (Pennsylvania); April 20, 1912 (Oregon and Nebraska); May 7, 1912 (Maryland); May 13, 1912 (Minnesota); May 15, 1912 (California); May 22, 1912 (Ohio); May 29, 1912 (New Jersey).

rect. By using his power over the party machinery, Taft was able to control the Republican convention which met at Chicago in June 1912 and win a second nomination for the presidency.[55]

Historians have wondered why Roosevelt decided to enter the presidential race in 1912, knowing as he did that defeat was probable. Less attention has been paid, however, to President Taft's decision to run for re-election, which was equally surprising. For almost no one believed in late 1911 and 1912 that Taft could be re-elected even if he managed to win the nomination. Not even his closest friends thought so, John O'Laughlin from the Washington Bureau of the Chicago *Tribune* discovered in December 1911. "Every man who is a candidate for office told me that if Taft should be the nominee, he would add no strength to his own particular candidacy. On the other hand he would have to carry the burden of Taft." [56] Even Taft himself saw no hope of victory and was impolitic enough to say so publicly in October 1911.[57] In the circumstances, one might have expected a graceful withdrawal by Taft rather than the stubborn fight he actually waged.

Equally significant and equally surprising is the amount of support Taft found among the regular Republicans for his candidacy. As the Roosevelt boom developed, many progressives counted on the political weakness of Taft to bring support to their cause from regular politicians anxious to climb on a promising band wagon. William Allen White's "wholesome respect for the acumen of the American politician" led him to the conviction in October 1911 that "in the end the Republican politician will dump Taft. For after all, the strongest political influence in America is the county ticket. You persuade the fellows at the courthouse that they are going to have a load on their necks with the presidential candidate, get it thoroughly in their noggins that any leader is a dead weight, and unless that leader happens to lead a mighty re-

---

[55] Mowry, *Theodore Roosevelt and the Progressive Movement,* pp. 237–252.

[56] J. C. O'Laughlin to Roosevelt, Dec. 10, 1911, Roosevelt Papers.

[57] New York *Times,* Oct. 31, 1911.

ligious cause, they will dump that leader." [58] As late as April 1912, Norris did not believe that the regulars would renominate Taft, even if they controlled the convention. "They certainly will not do this even if they can, unless they care more for the control of the party machinery than they do for the success of the party." [59]

But Norris and White were wrong. By and large, the Old Guard stuck by Taft throughout the contest, despite the acknowledged hopelessness of his cause. Certainly the Roosevelt movement attracted some conservative politicians anxious to find a popular candidate,[60] and talk of a third, compromise candidate was rife all through the early months of 1912.[61] At the convention itself some efforts were made by standpat politicians to draft Governor Herbert Hadley of Missouri, Roosevelt's floor manager at the convention, as a compromise candidate.[62] But considering the fact that a Democratic landslide was generally expected to follow the renomination of Taft, the most notable feature of the whole campaign was the remarkable firmness displayed by the Republican standpatters in standing by Taft to the bitter end. Taft's control of the party machinery through the presidential office was, of course, a vital factor in his victory. But presidential power alone was not enough to control a national convention, as Cleveland's failure to turn back the silver forces at the Democratic convention of 1896 had demonstrated. The second crucial factor in Taft's convention victory was the uncompromising resolution of the conservative Republican leadership to defeat the Roosevelt forces and renominate the President. "In 1912 the conservative Republicans were apparently quite willing to destroy the party and disappear rather than acquiesce in a pernicious progres-

---

[58] White to Roosevelt, Oct. 18, 1911, Roosevelt Papers.

[59] Norris to J. F. Sharp, April 27, 1912, Norris Papers.

[60] Mowry, *Theodore Roosevelt and the Progressive Movement*, pp. 202–203.

[61] New York *Times*, April 11, 1912.

[62] Mowry, *Theodore Roosevelt and the Progressive Movement*, pp. 250–252.

sivism," commented the *New Republic* some years later. "The Old Guard dies, but it doesn't surrender." [63]

The explanation of the standpatters' intransigence in 1912 is to be found in the provisos which Norris and White had appended to their predictions of a conservative defection from Taft. The courthouse politician would desert a hopeless candidate, White had written, unless that leader happens to lead a mighty religious cause, and the conservatives would not nominate Taft, in Norris's view, unless they care more for the control of the party machinery than they do for the success of the party. Unfortunately for the progressive Republicans, both of these provisions were fulfilled by the conditions of 1912.

The "mighty religious cause" was provided for the conservative Republicans, if it did not exist already, by Roosevelt's Columbus speech on February 21, 1912. In it Roosevelt spoke in favor of the recall of state judicial decisions, a step that most conservatives interpreted as an attack on the sanctity of the whole judicial system and a dangerous threat to American institutions.[64] Though Taft's administration had been "loosely conducted," Henry Cabot Lodge reported to Brooks Adams, "the errors that have been made . . . are lost sight of now, because Roosevelt's Columbus speech has turned Taft from a man into a principle." [65] Conservative and moderate Republicans who hitherto had had little enthusiasm for the President rushed to his support.[66]

As for the Old Guard's concern for controlling the party machinery even at the cost of losing the election, this was even more dramatically demonstrated in 1912 than it had been in 1910. Cannon reiterated his view that it would be better to have a Democrat in the White House than a man "who needs

---

[63] The *New Republic,* I, No. 11, Jan. 16, 1915.
[64] New York *Times,* Feb. 22, 1912.
[65] Henry Cabot Lodge to Brooks Adams, March 5, 1912, Henry Cabot Lodge Papers, Massachusetts Historical Society, Boston, Massachusetts.
[66] New York *Times,* Feb. 27, 1912.

an adjective to describe his Republicanism." [67] A Kansas standpat leader explained the conservative strategy this way: "We can't elect Taft but we are going to hold on to this organization and when we get back four years from now, we will have it and not those d——— insurgents." [68] A few years in retirement, another conservative observed, would give the Republican party a chance to rid itself of "our barnacles and political parasites." [69] Reminiscing in later years, Albert Beveridge recalled the "incredible high-handedness of the reactionaries who had control of the organization" at the 1912 convention: ". . . whatever was necessary to win, short of murder, they appeared to believe was permissible. It was anything to beat Roosevelt. Aside from the crude 'practical politician' point of view . . . there was the feeling on their part distinctly manifest, that it was necessary to 'save' the party from Roosevelt — he was a 'radical,' a 'socialist,' an 'anarchist,' etc." [70]

Within the inner circles of the Old Guard leadership this view was certainly the prevailing one. James Watson, the Indiana standpatter, tells in his memoirs how he and some other conservatives toyed with the idea of dropping Taft for a compromise candidate such as Herbert Hadley when the Old Guard leaders met at Chicago. But Boies Penrose, the boss of the Pennsylvania machine, expressed the dominant view. If it was a choice of losing control of the party and losing the election, Penrose advised, always lose the election. A few years of Democratic rule would inevitably result in the return of the Republican conservatives to power. But if Roosevelt took over control of the party machine, the power of the Old Guard might be shattered forever.[71] Penrose was firmly backed in this position by the other important conservative leaders. Elihu

[67] Joseph G. Cannon to George D. Perkins, August 11, 1911, Perkins Papers.

[68] David Mulvane, quoted by Walter Johnson, *William Allen White's America* (New York, 1947), p. 203.

[69] Henry H. Elliot to Knute Nelson, Sept. 29, 1912, Nelson Papers.

[70] Beveridge to White, Dec. 8, 1919, White Papers.

[71] James E. Watson, *As I Knew Them: Memoirs of James E. Watson* (Indianapolis, 1936), pp. 150–151. Slightly different versions of

Root expressed the view that the results of the convention were more important than the results of the election,[72] and William Barnes Jr., the boss of New York Republicans, declared that the primary purpose of the convention delegates had been "to preserve the political organism known as the Republican party as the safeguard of the individual liberty of every citizen of the United States." [73]

Nobody believed more firmly in the need to save the Republican party from the dangers of Rooseveltian radicalism than Taft himself. A "most serious menace to our Republican institutions has been averted," he declared after his victory at the convention.[74] Writing to Barnes a few days later, he expanded on this theme:

> I quite agree with you that the victory in November is by no means the most important purpose before us. It should be to retain the party and the principles of the party, so as to keep in a condition of activity and discipline a united force to strike when the blow will become effective for the retention of conservative government and conservative institutions and for the over-turning, should we have to meet it, of a Democratic administration. . . . It is the Republican party with its old principles that we must labor to maintain and keep vitalized and active. If victory comes next November, well and good; if it does not we shall know that in June we accomplished a great victory and that we are merely holding our forces in line for victories in the future to protect that which is valuable in our country's government.[75]

Three days previously, Jacob Gallinger, the Republican minority leader in the Senate, had visited the White House and

---

this story are told by two biographers of Boies Penrose: Robert Douglas Bowden, *Boies Penrose: Symbol of an Era* (New York, 1937), pp. 221–222; Walter Davenport, *Power and Glory: The Life of Boies Penrose* (New York, 1931), pp. 190–192.

[72] Elihu Root to S. H. Church, July 3, 1912, Elihu Root Papers, Library of Congress.

[73] William Barnes Jr., "The Future of the Republican Party," *Harpers' Weekly*, LVI, No. 2922, Dec. 21, 1912.

[74] New York *Times*, June 23, 1912.

[75] William Howard Taft to William Barnes Jr., Jan. 29, 1912, Taft Papers.

found Taft "fresh and happy. He says that the chief thing was accomplished in the defeat of Roosevelt, and that if he [Taft] is beaten, the organization will still exist." [76]

On this occasion at least, Taft's political judgement was not at fault. Certainly it took longer than the Old Guard had expected to bring the Republican party back to power after 1912. But when that moment arrived in 1920, the conservatives were firmly in control. The attempt of the progressives to seize control of the Republican party through the candidacy of Theodore Roosevelt failed in 1912, and the verdict proved to be final.

[76] Jacob Gallinger to J. O. Lyford, June 26, 1912, Jacob H. Gallinger Papers, New Hampshire Historical Society, Concord, New Hampshire.

# chapter five

# "A Pronounced Feeling of Regularity"

The failure of the Roosevelt forces to win control of the Republican party at the Chicago convention was followed immediately by an attempt to establish a third party — the Progressive or Bull Moose party — under the leadership of Theodore Roosevelt. In a way this formal split in the Republican party seemed only the logical culmination of the great intraparty battles of the Taft administration. By 1911 there were, in practice, three parties in Congress — Democrats, regular Republicans, and insurgent Republicans — and the depth of the division in the Republican party was demonstrated by the demands made in April 1911 by the insurgent Senators for what amounted to formal recognition of their own organization in the Senate.[1] The Senators had no intention of attempting to organize a third party outside Congress at this point, but some progressive Republicans were looking forward to the day when they would not have to share a party organization with the likes of Cannon and Aldrich. Gifford Pinchot, for instance, was talking about "the chance for a third party" in May 1911,[2] and his brother Amos was speculating on the possibility as early as December 1910. "This talk of pulling the

---

[1] See p. 46 above.
[2] Gifford Pinchot to Sir Horace Plunkett, May 27, 1911, Pinchot Papers.

party together makes me sick," he wrote to Beveridge.[3]

When Roosevelt decided to form the third party in 1912, it was men like the Pinchots who supported the move most enthusiastically. Not prairie state insurgents — but non-office-holding amateur politicians, social reformers, college professors, intellectuals, and urban dwellers very often from the social elite of the great northern cities — made up the bulk of the new party's leadership. Unlike the typical insurgent, the Bull Mooser generally was a man of little experience in national politics before 1912. In very few cases was he a power in his state Republican party, though he had normally been a nominal Republican before 1912. Roosevelt was as much bringing these men into politics as he was taking them out of the Republican party when he formed the new party.[4]

Among progressives who had worked for many years to establish themselves in the Republican party, the response to the new party was cool. Beveridge's immediate reactions were typical. Though everyone agreed on the need for "a frankly liberal and a frankly conservative party," he wrote in July 1912, it was "still on the knees of the Gods" whether a third party was the method for doing this. "Just at present I am doing and saying nothing." [5] Eventually Beveridge decided to throw in his lot with the third party, but significantly Beveridge was not in office in 1912. Most of the progressive Republicans who were in office elected to stay in the Republican party. They doubted whether the appeal of Roosevelt was enough in itself to establish the party on a permanent basis. They feared that the new party would merely split the Republican vote and lead to their defeat. They were reluctant to give up their hard-earned positions of power in the state parties. Writing to Roosevelt in July, Herbert Hadley, the progressive Republican governor of Missouri who had served as Roosevelt's floor leader

---

[3] Amos Pinchot to Beveridge, Nov. 25, 1910, Beveridge Papers.
[4] Alfred D. Chandler Jr., "The Origins of Progressive Leadership," Elting Morison (ed.), *The Letters of Theodore Roosevelt*, 8 vols. (Cambridge, Mass., 1954), VIII, 1462–1465.
[5] Beveridge to James W. Noel, July 12, 1912, Beveridge Papers.

at the Chicago convention, declined to join the new party:
"Our party here is progressive, and is in the control of those
who believe in right principles of government. While there is
a strong anti-Taft sentiment within the party, and a strong
sentiment for you, there is also a pronounced feeling of regu-
larity in this state which would make the work of organizing
a new party at this time a very difficult one." [6]

Of the progressive Republican Senators only Poindexter and
Dixon committed themselves to the Progressive party in 1912.[7]
In Dixon's state, Montana, the progressives had lost control of
the Republican organization in the April primaries, and it was
considered doubtful whether Dixon would be renominated at
the fall convention, so he had little to lose by accepting a Progressive nomination.[8] It seems likely that Dixon never had any
hope of winning back his Senate seat in the three-way race that
developed in Montana since he did not campaign at all there
and devoted himself entirely to his work as national chairman
of the Progressive party.[9] Poindexter had no more desire to
join the new party than his colleagues and advised his supporters not to do so.[10] But when the progressive Republicans

---

[6] Herbert Hadley to Roosevelt, July 5, 1912, Roosevelt Papers.

[7] Mowry, in *Theodore Roosevelt and the Progressive Movement,* p.
257, states that Bristow and Clapp joined the third party in 1912.
Though some press reports did suggest this, such as one in the Des
Moines *Register,* July 4, 1912, in fact the position of these two Senators was no different from that of Cummins at this time. That is,
they endorsed Roosevelt for President but made no commitment to
the Progressive party. Clapp did begin to align himself publicly with
the Progressive party late in 1913, but in 1912 he avoided any such
commitment. See Minneapolis *Journal,* Sept. 28, 1913. Bristow flirted
with the third party for some months after the 1912 election, but
at no stage did he commit himself to it, and before the end of 1913
he had decided definitely to remain a Republican. See Bristow to
George M. Hull, June 25, 1912, Bristow Papers, for his position before the 1912 election.

[8] Helena *Independent,* May 12, 1912.

[9] *Ibid.,* Sept. 8, 1912.

[10] Poindexter to G. A. Haynes, July 11, 1912, Poindexter Papers;
New York *Times,* July 7, 1912.

in Washington state disregarded his advice and bolted the party, Poindexter felt obliged to follow.[11]

It is more difficult to generalize about the positive response of the insurgents to the new situation. Certainly they did not present a united front. A conference of insurgent Senators called by Albert Cummins on July 4 failed to come to any conclusion as to what ought to be done.[12] Many issued ambiguous statements deploring the outcome of the Chicago convention but stating that they were still Republicans. One insurgent Congressman from Wisconsin wrote to a colleague that he had decided to make no speeches at all during the campaign for fear of alienating either Taft or Roosevelt supporters.[13] Senator Borah of Idaho received the support of the state Bull Moosers and greeted Roosevelt when the latter arrived in Boise on a campaign trip, but he did not endorse either Roosevelt or Taft.[14] Senator Works of California supported Wilson.[15] Others, such as Senator Clapp of Minnesota, endorsed Roosevelt's candidacy but failed to make it clear what their relationship would be to his new party.[16] The California progressives decided to remain Republicans in their state where they controlled the party machinery, but Progressives

---

[11] Howard W. Allen, "Miles Poindexter and the Progressive Movement," *Pacific Northwest Quarterly,* July 1962, pp. 117–118. In his unpublished biography *Poindexter,* Howard W. Allen notes that it was the progressive Republicans from the western part of Washington state who were most enthusiastic about forming a third party, though traditionally the eastern areas had been the center of radicalism (p. 187). This emphasizes the fact that the third party issue was not a question of radicals versus the less radical but the established versus the less established. Being further removed from political power than the eastern progressives in Washington, the westerners were more eager to experiment with the new party.

[12] Cummins to Bristow, July 1, 1912, Bristow papers; New York *Times,* June 26, 1912; Des Moines *Register,* July 4, 1912.

[13] James H. Davidson to J. J. Esch, Oct. 7, 1912, Esch Papers.

[14] Johnson, *Borah,* p. 141; Des Moines *Register,* Sept. 13, 1912; Borah to Bristow, Sept. 23, 1912, Bristow Papers.

[15] New York *Times,* Sept. 24, 1912.

[16] Minneapolis *Journal,* Sept. 28, 1913.

nationally.[17] The total situation remained confused, even cha-
otic, and newspaper reports of the period often prove to be
contradictory and unreliable.[18]

However, a fairly clear pattern gradually emerged in the
agrarian middle-western states where the progressive Republican movement was strongest: Iowa, Wisconsin, Minnesota,
Kansas, Nebraska, and the Dakotas. Most of the progressive
Republican leaders from these states endorsed Roosevelt for
president, but practically without exception they refused to
leave the Republican party in 1912.[19] There was of course no
possibility of Robert La Follette following Theodore Roosevelt into the third party, or indeed, anywhere else. La Follette
was reported at times to be favoring Wilson, but he announced
late in the campaign that he would not support any candidate
for the presidency.[20] Wisconsin's Governor, Francis E. McGovern, announced that he would vote for Roosevelt, but he remained a Republican and supported the whole state Republican ticket.[21] The Progressive party made no nominations for
state or national offices in Wisconsin except for the presidential ticket.[22]

In Kansas, where the progressives controlled the Republican
party organization in 1912, it was decided not to form a third
party before the November election. There was no point in a
third party where progressives already were in control, Governor Stubbs declared after the bolt at Chicago. "The third
party is to be formed only in 'stand-pat' states." [23] William

---

[17] George E. Mowry, *The California Progressives* (Berkeley, Cal.,
1951), p. 188.

[18] New York *Times,* Oct. 28, 1912.

[19] Many of the Kansas progressives including Victor Murdock, William R. Stubbs, and William Allen White did join the third party
after the general defeat of the Kansas progressive Republicans by
Democrats in the 1912 elections. But up to the time of the election
they stayed within the Republican party.

[20] Des Moines *Register,* Oct. 26, 1912.

[21] Kansas City *Star,* Sept. 27, 1912.

[22] General election data was drawn largely from the *New York
Tribune Almanac* for 1913.

[23] New York *Times,* June 25, 1912.

Allen White and all the other important state progressive leaders agreed. "The rank and file of the everyday Republicans in Kansas have a right to their party machinery, and they propose to hold it," White editorialized in July.[24] "I see no occasion whatever for a third party in Kansas, and hope none will be formed," Senator Bristow wrote.[25] In the state primary elections held in August, the progressives nominated their candidates for Governor and U. S. Senator, Arthur Capper and Governor Stubbs, on the Republican ticket, together with a slate of Roosevelt electors. Later it was decided to place the presidential electors in an independent column, thereby allowing Taft a place on the ballot,[26] but there were no Progressive candidates for other offices in Kansas in 1912.

In South Dakota the progressives who controlled the state Republican party went so far as to exclude Taft from the ballot entirely by placing a slate of Roosevelt electors in the Republican column. There was no Progressive party in South Dakota in 1912.[27] In North Dakota there was a Progressive candidate for the Governorship but for no other office, since that was the only office not controlled by the progressive Republicans.[28] In Nebraska Governor Aldrich announced that there was "no occasion for a new party"; for the progressives were in control of the G.O.P., and a bolt would simply "throw the Republican machinery into the hands of the reactionaries."[29] Norris, running for the Senate in 1912, also took this position.[30] A Bull Moose organization was established, but it endorsed Governor Aldrich and the whole state Republican ticket with a single exception.[31] In Minnesota the Progressive

---

[24] Kansas City *Star,* July 7, 1912.
[25] Bristow to J. R. Harrison, July 22, 1912, Bristow Papers.
[26] New York *Times,* August 7, 1912; Kansas City *Star,* August 18, 1912; *ibid.,* August 27, 1912; Des Moines *Register,* Sept. 19, 1912.
[27] John Sutherland to Coe Crawford, July 29, 1912, Crawford Papers; Armin, *Crawford,* p. 277.
[28] Phillips, *Gronna,* Chapter 6.
[29] New York *Times,* June 25, 1912.
[30] Norris to F. P. Corrick, August 31, 1912, Norris Papers.
[31] New York *Times,* Sept. 5, 1912.

party made a more significant effort by nominating candidates for Governor, Secretary of State, railroad and warehouse commissioners, and two congressional seats. But it offered no candidates in seven other congressional districts.[32]

The situation in Iowa seemed at first to be developing along the same lines as in the other states where Republican insurgency had been dominant in the Taft years. Early in July Senator Cummins, the leader of the state's progressive Republicans, announced that he would continue to fight for progressivism within the Republican party. While he deeply regretted the dishonest and unfair practices which had characterized the Chicago convention, he said he could not believe "that our disappointment, however profound, or the dishonesty of individuals, however heinous, can constitute a foundation upon which to rear a new party." [33] A few days later a Bull Moose organization was established in Iowa, but its leader, Judge John L. Stevens, announced that only a national ticket would be presented and that there would be no interference with the re-election bids of Senator Kenyon or the state Republican ticket.[34]

By mid-August, however, the Iowa Bull Moosers were threatening to run a full state ticket in the November elections unless the Republican nominees who were sitting on the fence between Taft and Roosevelt openly endorsed the national Progressive party ticket.[35] Senator Cummins responded by declaring that he would support Roosevelt if he could do so without leaving the Republican party, but Senator Kenyon announced that he would support the entire Republican ticket.[36] The day after Kenyon's statement the Iowa Progressive party decided to enter a full ticket in the campaign, a decision which one committeeman said sprang from disgust

---

[32] Des Moines *Register,* Oct. 6, 1912.
[33] New York *Times,* July 6, 1912.
[34] Des Moines *Register,* July 9, 1912.
[35] *Ibid.,* August 16, 1912.
[36] New York *Times,* August 22, 1912; Des Moines *Register,* August 21, 1912.

with Senator Kenyon's statement.[37] Others attributed the decision to the pressure of Medill McCormick from the Progressive party's national committee, who was in Des Moines urging a full state ticket at this time.[38] The Bull Moosers nominated a full ticket for the state offices and contested eight out of eleven congressional seats.[39] However, though the third party did organize seriously in Iowa in 1912, the established progressive Republican leadership remained inside the Republican party.

It becomes clear from all this that the Progressive party of 1912 was by no means a direct lineal descendant of the progressive Republican movement of the Taft administration. Between June and November of 1912 the two groups cooperated to some extent in a loose and uneasy alliance, but the distinction remained clear. Nor did the failure of the third party in the November elections mean the collapse of progressivism in the Republican party as has sometimes been argued.[40] In Congress, for instance, the progressive Republicans largely maintained their strength, and what losses occurred had little to do with the Bull Moose party. In Minnesota, Wisconsin, Nebraska, and the Dakotas the congressional delegations remained largely intact in 1912, and consequently largely progressive Republican. Only in Iowa did a third-party ticket split the Republican vote and help defeat two Republican congressmen.[41] In Kansas, the one insurgent state where progressive Republicans were badly defeated in 1912 by Democrats, there were no Bull Moosers running, and it is hard to see how the third party could have affected the results. Stubbs running for the Senate, Capper running for Governor, and three incumbent Congressmen were defeated by Democrats in straight two-party contests with no third-party complications.[42]

---

37 *Ibid.*, August 22, 1912.
38 Bristow to William Allen White, Dec. 3, 1912, White Papers.
39 *New York Tribune Almanac,* 1913, pp. 697–698.
40 Mowry makes this argument in *Theodore Roosevelt and the Progressive Movement,* especially pp. 208, 252, 282–283.
41 *New York Tribune Almanac,* 1913, p. 698.
42 *Ibid.,* p. 699.

Of the two progressive Republican Senators defeated in 1912, only Dixon can be accounted a casualty of the third party, and as we have seen, he had joined the new party after it had become probable that the state Republican party would refuse to renominate him.[43] The other, Bourne of Oregon, was defeated in the Republican primaries before the bolt took place. Bourne had made no campaign at all and had not visited his state for two years prior to this defeat.[44]

There is indeed some reason to believe that Roosevelt's presidential campaign actually strengthened the position of progressive Republicans in the 1912 elections. Much of the maneuvering of midwestern progressive Republicans between 1909 and 1912 had amounted to an attempt to dissociate themselves from the disastrous political burden of Aldrich, Cannon, and Taft. By 1911 most of them were convinced that their only chance of surviving the elections of the following year was to persuade their constituents that their Republicanism was something quite different from that of the President. Most of La Follette's backers had this consideration in mind when they supported his presidential campaign against odds that most agreed were hopeless.[45] Similarly Roosevelt's third-party candidacy gave the progressives something to cling to after June 1912. Though Roosevelt was the nominee of a third party, progressive Republicans could and did claim him as the true Republican candidate, thereby saving themselves to some extent from a disastrous association in the public mind with Taft.

Although most of the leading insurgents had refused to join the third party before the election, the Bull Moosers had confidently expected many of them to do so after it. But the poor performances of the Progressive candidates other than Roosevelt himself in the November elections confirmed most of the insurgent leaders in their view that the safest course of action was to remain inside the Republican party. Poindexter was

---

[43] See p. 65 above.
[44] Pike, *Bourne*, pp. 171–185.
[45] See pp. 48–50.

the only Senator to list himself as a Progressive in the Congressional Directory in the Sixty-third Congress, which met in 1913, and only five of the old insurgents in the House designated themselves Progressives or Progressive Republicans. The other dozen or so Progressive party congressmen were all newcomers, most of them from states that had been normally controlled by conservative Republicans before 1912.[46] The California progressives, led by Governor Hiram Johnson, were the only entrenched group of Republican progressives who decided after the 1912 elections to move bag and baggage into the new party.[47] They remained a unique group in the next few years, being the only Bull Moosers to win substantial victories in the 1914 elections and maintain their strength throughout the short life of the third party.[48] In 1916 the California progressives moved en bloc back into the Republican party and once again dominated its organization as they had done before 1912.[49]

Among the progressive Republicans in the middle west, however, there was no rush to affiliate with the new party. Only in Kansas did an important section of the established progressive Republican leadership embrace the Progressive party in 1913, and it is suggestive that the Kansas progressives were the one group of midwestern insurgents which had been badly defeated in the 1912 elections. Even in Kansas the progressives were not united on the issue of the third party. Ex-Governor Stubbs, Congressman Victor Murdock, and William Allen White were all in favor of joining the Progressive party at this stage;[50] but Arthur Capper, who had lost the race for the Governorship in 1912, and Senator Bristow, who faced re-election in 1914, were at first doubtful and then openly hostile to the idea.

---

[46] *La Follette's Weekly*, V, No. 15, April 12, 1913. There were five from Pennsylvania, two from Illinois, one from New York, and one from Michigan.

[47] Mowry, *California Progressives*, pp. 196–198.

[48] *Ibid.*, p. 218.

[49] *Ibid.*, p. 278.

[50] White to W. R. Stubbs, Jan. 6, 1914, White Papers.

Capper thought that Wilson's early successes had made a third party impossible.[51] Bristow's doubts sprang not from any fear that the Bull Moose party was too radical but from a conviction that the third-party movement was a tactical blunder which would lead to his defeat in 1914. At no stage was he enthusiastic about the Progressive party, suggesting the organization of progressive clubs rather than a Progressive party in Kansas after the 1912 election.[52] However, Arthur Capper was soon writing to Bristow (who was in Washington throughout the key period when the Progressive party was being organized in Kansas) that the prevailing opinion in the state was in favor of the new party.[53] Apparently resigned to this development, Bristow replied that although he would have preferred to stay inside the Republican party "so as to get advantage of the ten to twenty thousand votes which are cast for the old ticket regardless of who is on it," he hoped that the new party would be organized quickly and effectively if it was going to be done.[54]

Through the early months of 1913 Bristow moved hesitantly, attempting to cooperate with the sponsors of the Bull Moose party without alienating his Republican supporters.[55] But by the late summer of 1913 he was convinced that the third party was collapsing nationally, and he was growing more and more concerned about those "ten to twenty thousand votes," which later grew to fifty thousand in his estimation.[56] In January 1914 Bristow announced his intention of running for re-election as a Republican.[57] White and the Progressives were incensed at this "treachery" of Bristow and countered by running Victor Murdock for the Senate and Henry Allen (against Capper) for Governor on the Progressive ticket. Attacked by Mur-

---

[51] Arthur Capper to White, Oct. 11, 1913, *ibid.*
[52] Bristow to White, Dec. 2, 1912, Bristow Papers.
[53] Capper to Bristow, Dec. 5, 1912, *ibid.*
[54] Bristow to Capper, Dec. 8, 1912, *ibid.*
[55] Bristow to John Madden, April 7, 1913, *ibid.*
[56] Bristow to Joseph M. Dixon, August 25, 1913, *ibid.*; White to Hageman, Feb. 16, 1914, White Papers.
[57] *La Follette's Weekly,* VI, No. 2, Jan. 10, 1914.

dock and the Progressives on the one hand and the Kansas Old Guard on the other, Bristow was defeated in the Republican primaries by Charles Curtis, the same standpatter whom Stubbs had beaten in 1912.[58] In the general elections Curtis went on to defeat Allen, with Bristow campaigning for Curtis against the third party. Capper was luckier than Bristow, being unopposed by a conservative in the primaries, and was elected Governor in 1914.

The Kansas debacle in 1914 was the outstanding case of third-party activity causing the defeat of progressive Republicans who had been well-established prior to 1912. "I am perfectly willing to admit," said William Allen White, "that Capper and Bristow were right in contending that in union under the Republican banner we could have won, if they are willing to admit that under the Progressive banner, we could have won. But it is evident that neither one of us could win very much under a divided banner." [59] Even in Kansas, however, the Bull Moose episode did not permanently destroy progressivism in the Republican party. Arthur Capper, elected Governor in 1914, was re-elected in 1916 and went on to the Senate in 1918, where he remained for 30 years. Henry Allen, defeated as the Bull Moose candidate for Governor in 1914, won the office as a Republican in 1918.[60]

Outside Kansas the Bull Moosers took no greater toll of progressive Republicans in 1914 than they had done in 1912, although this was not for lack of effort on their part. Through 1913 the Bull Moosers had been merely puzzled and upset at the attitude of the progressive Republican leaders toward their party. "I *do* wish Cummins would come over to us," Beveridge lamented in June. "He belongs to us, and I am so very fond of him. Why *will* he persist in fiddling along trying to patch

---

[58] New York *Times,* Jan. 20, 1914; *ibid.,* August 6 and 7, 1914.

[59] White to Roy Bailey, Nov. 17, 1914, White Papers.

[60] Alfred M. Landon, who was a county chairman for the Progressive party in Kansas in 1914, believes that Bristow was the only major casualty of the split in the progressive ranks in Kansas from 1913 to 1914. Interview, May 8, 1963.

up the unpatchable?" [61] Senator Clapp, who took the unusual course of moving closer to the Progressive party in 1913, was equally bewildered by the refusal of Cummins to abandon the G.O.P. "At Trenton a short time ago, in an address, he plainly told them that the Chicago crime could neither be condoned nor forgotten and yet, strangely enough, . . . he seeks to reconcile these forces." [62]

By the end of the year this dismay had turned to anger. In December Beveridge was saying that the so-called progressive Republicans were more dangerous than open reactionaries.[63] O. K. Davis, the Executive Secretary of the Progressive party, asked for a strong attack on the attempt of the "Cummins-Borah crowd" to reorganize the Republican party.[64] The primary purpose of the Progressive party for 1914, William Allen White wrote in February, should be "to make it absolutely impossible for any so-called Progressive Republican to return to either house of Congress or to sit as governor." With this in mind, White added, Victor Murdock was taking a few days off from his campaign in Kansas to organize a Bull Moose candidacy against Cummins in Iowa.[65] The extent and character of the Progressive party's growth in 1914, another Bull Mooser thought, would depend on events in Kansas, Nebraska, Iowa, the two Dakotas, and Minnesota. "In all but two of them, there are progressive Republicans, so-called, up for re-election to the Senate. The defeat of these men will contribute more than anything else to the enhancement of our strength." A major effort was especially needed to defeat the progressive Republican Senator from South Dakota, Coe Crawford "and his gang of Janus-headed political invertebrates." [66]

But the Progressives failed to dislodge Cummins or any

[61] Beveridge to Moses E. Clapp, June 27, 1913, Beveridge Papers.
[62] Clapp to Beveridge, July 1, 1913, *ibid.*
[63] Beveridge to Julian S. Mason, Dec. 4, 1913, *ibid.*
[64] O. K. Davis to George W. Perkins, Nov. 16, 1913, *ibid.*
[65] White to Roosevelt, Feb. 7, 1914, White Papers.
[66] Medill McCormick (?) to O. K. Davis, Feb. 21, 1914, Beveridge Papers.

other prominent progressive Republican save Bristow in 1914. Though Crawford was defeated in South Dakota, this had nothing to do with the Bull Moosers, who did not field a candidate against him. Crawford's biographer attributes his defeat in the Republican primary of 1914 to neglect of constituents, poor organization, the personal appeal of his stalwart opponent, and a certain coolness on the part of progressive and rural voters to his defections from the insurgent ranks in the past.[67] Whatever happened to progressive Republicanism, it was not destroyed by the Bull Moose.[68]

Having failed to absorb the old Republican insurgent movement, the Progressive party was left without any solid political base, dependent for its survival almost entirely on the personal appeal of its leader, Theodore Roosevelt. In a political system as decentralized as that of the United States, such a dependence was bound to prove fatal. After the 1912 election when

[67] Armin, *Crawford,* pp. 293–300.

[68] Apart from those political figures already discussed, Mowry mentions two other progressive Republicans who were "caught in the cross-fire between Progressives and Republicans" and defeated, Senators Moses E. Clapp and John D. Works (Mowry, *Theodore Roosevelt and the Progressive Movement,* p. 378). Works retired from the Senate in 1916 without a contest and was replaced by Hiram Johnson, a Republican who was more deeply committed to progressive reform than Works had ever been. See New York *Times,* August 30 and 31. Clapp was defeated in the Republican primaries in June 1916 after the Progressive party had passed out of existence. (New York *Times,* June 24, 1916.) He ran third in the race behind Frank B. Kellogg and Governor Adolph D. Eberhart. It is possible that Clapp's position was weakened by his dalliance with the Progressive party from 1913 to 1916. But local newspapers cited other reasons for the defeat of Clapp, especially his antipreparedness stand, which Kellogg attacked vigorously. Another factor would seem to have been Kellogg's well-financed and thorough campaign. Kellogg had the backing of most of the state's newspapers, campaigned aggressively in every district, and placed many large advertisements in the newspapers. By contrast, Clapp campaigned very little and had visited the state only a few times in the previous ten years. In any case, Clapp was certainly not caught in any cross fire. Minneapolis *Journal,* June 18 and June 20, 1916; Minneapolis *Morning Tribune,* April 1, and June 20, 1916.

Roosevelt had polled more votes than Taft, many Progressives compared their situation to that of the Republican party in 1856 when that new party established itself as the second party in the nation. Theodore Roosevelt himself pointed out the flaw in this analogy. The Republicans, he noted, knocked out the Whigs and took control of Congress *before* their first great national leader emerged.[69] But in 1912 most Progressive candidates for state and local offices ran well behind Roosevelt's vote, and in 1914, without his name at the head of the ticket, they were slaughtered at the polls everywhere except California, where a deeply rooted group of ex-insurgents controlled the party.

Looking back at the Bull Moose experiment in 1916, William Allen White concluded that the Progressive party had never really functioned as a party in the ordinary sense at all. They had been a group of agitators without enough genuine officeseekers wanting political jobs for their own sake.[70] Three years earlier White had foreseen that the Progressive party would have difficulty holding the votes polled by Roosevelt in 1912. The party would lose the "sheep" votes, he said — voters influenced chiefly by tradition and noise. The noise had subsided after 1912, and tradition would pull them back to the Republicans. Also they would lose the "Teddy" votes — personal admirers of Roosevelt. White had originally thought that Roosevelt ought not to run again in 1916, in order "to demonstrate that we were not a one-man party," but he had changed his mind because Roosevelt's popularity was "a political fact that we cannot ignore." [71] In other words the Progressive party *was* a one-man party.

Most of the other difficulties faced by the Bull Moosers also stemmed from their dependence on Roosevelt. There was, for instance, the problem of what to do about George Perkins, the party's executive secretary, its financial god-father, and its effective leader in matters of day-to-day management. The

---

[69] Roosevelt to White, Nov. 7, 1914, Roosevelt Papers.
[70] White to Gifford Pinchot, June 23, 1916, White Papers.
[71] White to Roosevelt, Sept. 24, 1913, *ibid.*

trouble with Perkins, as William Allen White said, "isn't the fact that Perkins is a Wall St. man; it isn't the fact that he feels he should defend the Steel trust and the Harvester trust in the bulletin; it isn't the fact that he is generally supposed to have backed up O. K. [Davis — the party's executive secretary] in swiping the objectionable [anti-trust] planks of the platform; it isn't the fact that Perkins was a former partner of Morgan's." It was rather that "no man should long continue as the real active, managerial head of the party — particularly unassisted or directed by anyone — who combines all the points of attacks that Perkins combines." [72] Sentiments such as these were widespread in the Progressive ranks and led to an open flare-up in 1914 when Perkins' most trenchant opponent, Amos Pinchot, sent a letter to every member of the party's executive committee denouncing Perkins and demanding he be ousted. The letter became public knowledge and gave the party much unfavorable publicity on the eve of the vital midterm elections.[73]

There is little doubt that anti-Perkins sentiment was general throughout the Progressive party in 1914, yet Perkins remained in his powerful post throughout the party's life and was never really in serious danger of losing it. In part Perkins owed his security to the dependence of the party on his financial resources and managerial abilities, but even more to the point was the fact that he had the complete confidence of Theodore Roosevelt. When Roosevelt said that if Perkins left the party he would leave also, the anti-Perkins movement quickly faded away.[74] It was impossible for a Bull Mooser to attack Roosevelt or even to conceive of the party without him.

Some of the vehemence with which men like Pinchot attacked Perkins arose from this very fact. Every Bull Mooser did not agree with Roosevelt on every question of policy and

---

[72] White to Beveridge, July 31, 1914, Beveridge Papers.
[73] Mowry, *Theodore Roosevelt and the Progressive Movement,* pp. 294–298.
[74] New York *Times,* June 25, 1914.

strategy, but since the chief himself was politically indispensable and therefore unassailable, attacks had to be made on subordinates like Perkins who represented some aspect of Roosevelt's views. "What is the objection to George Perkins?" queried Albert Beveridge. "Surely it cannot be his economic views on the trust question [as Pinchot was saying], for they are precisely those of Colonel Roosevelt." [75] This was undoubtedly true, but how could a Bull Mooser attack the public views of Theodore Roosevelt?

The frustration of the Progressive rank-and-file reached even greater heights in 1915 and 1916 when the major issue facing the party was whether to amalgamate with the Republicans on the best possible terms or to go ahead with an independent presidential candidacy in 1916. The radicals wanted Roosevelt to run as a Progressive if he could not get the Republican nomination, but their position was fatally weak since it depended entirely on the personal whim of Roosevelt himself. Within a major party a dissident faction ordinarily would gather around the candidacy of a man willing to run on its platform. But in this peculiar one-man party, the radicals, though they dominated the national convention in 1916, could only try to pressure their indispensable leader into the actions they wanted. When he declined to run, the party simply folded up.[76] Twenty-five years later a leading Bull Mooser intimately involved in the events of 1916, Harold Ickes, was still blaming Perkins for the death of the Progressive party. Ickes attributed the whole amalgamation strategy to Perkins, who he said had misled and misguided Roosevelt.[77] But this was the same self-deception that so many Bull Moosers displayed at the time. Perkins was not the evil genius of the Progressive party but merely the instrument of Roosevelt. The idea of an independ-

---

[75] Beveridge to White, July 6, 1914, Beveridge Papers.
[76] Mowry, *Theodore Roosevelt and the Progressive Movement*, pp. 347–355.
[77] Harold Ickes, "Who Killed the Progressive Party," *American Historical Review*, XLVI, No. 2, Jan. 1941, 306–337.

ent candidacy had been rejected by Roosevelt at least a year before the presidential conventions were held, and by this decision Roosevelt had condemned the Progressive party to death.[78]

---

[78] Mowry, *Theodore Roosevelt and the Progressive Movement,* p. 323.

# chapter six

# Wilson and the Underwood Tariff

Throughout the years of the Taft administration the insurgents had rarely left the center of the political stage. But in 1913 they suddenly found themselves overshadowed by the Democratic progressives, who with Woodrow Wilson in the presidency had achieved that national power that continually eluded their Republican counterparts. Nor did the progressive Republicans retain the legislative influence which they had been able to wield so effectively under Taft, for with clear Democratic majorities in both the House and the Senate, the insurgents no longer held the balance of legislative power in Congress. In addition, the existence of the new Progressive party, while it had done little to weaken the progressive Republican movement on its home ground, did threaten to limit the spread of progressivism in the Republican party on a national scale.

Despite these limiting factors, the insurgents were not a negligible political force at the beginning of the Wilson era. With 30 or 40 Representatives and 10 to 12 Senators in Congress, they might still hope to play a significant role in national politics. This was particularly so in the Senate, for there the insurgents could boast of an extraordinary array of oratorical, intellectual, and general parliamentary talent for such a small group. A force which included Robert La Follette, William Borah, George Norris, Albert Cummins, and Joseph Bristow would have been formidable in any Congressional debate. More generally, the future actions of the insurgent Republicans would perhaps be a crucial factor in the development of the whole progressive movement and the party system henceforth. Would they lean toward Wilson and help bring about a realignment of parties based on ideological divisions? Would they find some new working relationship with the Republican stalwarts and thereby mend the party split which had helped bring the Democrats to power? Or would they flirt once more with Theodore Roosevelt, perhaps seeking to make him the Republican presidential candidate for 1916, as they had done in 1912?

In the early months of 1913 a number of rumors floating around the capital suggested that a Republican-Democratic coalition of progressives was emerging. In January, for instance, it was reported that Wilson was considering appointing Republican Senator-elect George W. Norris to his cabinet as Secretary of the Interior.[1] In March a visit to the White House by La Follette was heralded by the New York *Times* as a "revolution in politics" and an indication that "under the Democratic Administration this Republican Senator will have as much to say about the party politics of the Democracy as any Democrat." [2]

But these speculations were based on the logical possibilities of the situation rather than objective realities. It seemed to contemporary observers, as it has to more recent historians, that in 1913 Wilson had an opportunity to draw all the progressives into one party organization.[3] In the 1912 election, Wilson had been endorsed by one insurgent Senator, and none of the others had been strongly opposed to him.[4] Ideologically

[1] New York *Times,* Jan. 10, 1913.

[2] *Ibid.,* March 14, 1913.

[3] John M. Blum, *Woodrow Wilson and the Politics of Morality* (Boston, 1956), p. 66; Arthur S. Link, *Wilson: The New Freedom* (Princeton, 1956), p. 153.

[4] The Senator who endorsed Wilson was Works of California. Mowry, *Theodore Roosevelt and the Progressive Movement,* p. 257, states that La Follette and Gronna also supported Wilson in 1912, but this appears to be incorrect. La Follette published a pro-Wilson article by Works in his magazine but did not openly endorse the

the insurgents were clearly closer to Wilson than to the Republican Old Guard, or even to Roosevelt. Although they were generally suspicious of Roosevelt's regulatory doctrines, they saw Woodrow Wilson's *New Freedom* as "a splendid enunciation of fundamental principles," to quote Senator Clapp.[5] Yet, in fact, there was no party realignment in the Wilson years, and before very long the progressive Republicans were to become as bitter critics of Wilson as the conservatives of their party.

An outright movement of incumbent progressive Republicans into the Democratic party was out of the question to begin with. Even those liberal Republicans who, twenty years later, endorsed Franklin Roosevelt for election and re-election, supported most of his programs, and accepted his executive patronage, did not go so far as to run for office under the Democratic label. In British politics, a major politician who changes his party allegiance can be found a new safe constituency should his previous electorate seem unlikely to follow him into the new party. But the American politician is tied to his home district or state, and must take his old supporters with him in any such adventure. The difficulty of this task is attested to by the very small number of politicians who have accomplished or even attempted it. A large proportion of the voters can be expected to vote for the regular party nominee, no matter who he is. To throw away these votes by changing party labels would have been a foolhardy maneuver, as Bristow kept insisting when he was under pressure to run for re-election in 1914 as a Progressive. It was doubly dangerous for the progressive Republicans, because they mostly came from states where the Republican party was traditionally dominant and where the Democrats seldom won. In any case there seemed no necessity to change party labels, because even if Wilson turned out to be an admirably progressive President his programs could be supported from the Republican side of the Congress. The

Democratic candidate himself. La Follette, *La Follette*, pp. 445, 450. For Gronna, see Phillips, *Gronna*, p. 317.

[5] *Cong. Record,* 63 Cong., 2 Session, Oct. 2, 1914, p. 16053.

most that could have been expected in 1913 was a general leaning of progressive Republicans toward the Wilson administration along the lines followed later by the Republican liberals of the 1930's, many of them the same individuals.

Even this did not occur in 1913. The first and most important reason was that Wilson as President made no real effort to cultivate the support of the progressive Republican leaders. Though he did try with some success to woo progressive Republican voters, especially in 1916, he did not attempt to draw the progressive Republican politicians themselves into his coalition as Franklin Roosevelt did later. Unlike Cleveland before him and Roosevelt afterwards, Wilson did not appoint a single Republican to his cabinet.[6] Insurgent Republican Senators did not receive executive patronage or electoral support as they did later under the New Deal. Above all, in his dealings with Congress, Wilson chose to work almost entirely through the Democratic organizations of the House and the Senate.

Perhaps a strictly partisan policy was the only practical one for Wilson. As John M. Blum has suggested, Wilson might well have lost more votes among the Democrats in Congress than he could have gained among the Republicans had he shown partiality to the progressive wing of the G.O.P.[7] Certainly the results of his chosen policy of working through Democrats and Democrats alone were impressive, especially in view of the disunity and lack of direction which had characterized the Democratic party up to this time. However, Wilson's reliance on the Democratic leadership and the Democratic caucus in Congress destroyed any chance there might have been for an entente between the progressive elements of the two major parties.

The emergence of the Democratic caucus as the real source of legislative power in the Congress was particularly galling to the insurgents. In their view centralized legislative organizations like party caucuses were synonymous with reactionary

---

[6] Link, *The New Freedom,* Chapter 1, *passim.*
[7] Blum, *Wilson,* p. 66.

policies. Their whole political experience, from the machines they had fought in their home states to Cannonism and Aldrichism in the Congress, had taught them this. They conceived of a caucus as a place where nefarious pressures were placed upon otherwise honest, progressive, independent legislators, never admitting that Wilson used the caucus to pressure conservatives as well as progressives. Even before Wilson had been inaugurated, La Follette was proclaiming that "the existing tyrannical caucus system must be supplanted if we are to have real progress." [8]

Far from supplanting the caucus, Wilson relied upon it as his prime instrument of legislative power. Agreements on administration programs were hammered out in the Democratic Congressional caucuses and then steam-rollered through Congress by solid Democratic majorities. In the standing committees Republican Congressmen and Senators, whether progressives or conservatives, were rarely allowed to play any significant part in the legislative process. The insurgent Republicans were outraged by these proceedings and quickly leapt to the assault. Their public speeches and private letters harped continuously on the evils of the Democratic caucuses, and to defeat them became an end in itself to many progressive Republicans. The destruction of the Democratic caucus would mean "the dawning of a better day," Senator Clapp wrote to Beveridge.[9]

As the prime mover behind the tightly organized Democratic legislative process, President Wilson also came under fire. "I regard President Wilson as an enemy of the constitution of the United States," Senator Cummins declared, "because of the big-stick methods which he employed in compelling the passage of the Underwood-Simmons tariff bill." [10] Senator Works thought it most unfortunate that the President, as head of the executive branch, should have a legislative program at all.[11] Bristow saw Wilson's use of patronage to reward

---

[8] *La Follette's Weekly,* IV, No. 45, Nov. 9, 1912.

[9] Clapp to Beveridge, Sept. 4, 1913, Beveridge Papers.

[10] New York *Times,* Oct. 31, 1913.

[11] *Cong. Record,* 63 Cong., 2 Session, July 17, 1914, p. 12282.

those who supported his bills as "a menace to free institutions." [12] The insurgents were continuously bemoaning the servility of the congressional Democrats to Wilson and the caucus. Senator Clapp saw them as a pliable group willing to say Amen to everything Wilson happened to propose.[13] He had never seen anything like Wilson's first Congress for "subserviency, abject and humiliating," Bristow remarked.[14] "I wish I were home," Borah wrote in the middle of a hot summer session, "but the Lord knows when we will get away and I am not sure that he would be permitted to determine the question until he had consulted the President." [15]

Quite apart from legislative matters, the insurgents became severe critics of every partisan aspect of the Wilson administration. From a very early date they began criticizing Wilson's appointments and attacking alleged attempts to set aside the civil service system.[16] They were continuously trying to embarrass the administration with charges of malign influences in various government departments and bills to reduce the appointive powers of the President.[17] As the *New Republic* commented, Wilson's "scrupulous loyalty to his own party and his determination to govern by means of a party machine and the use of partisan discipline has resulted in the recrudescence of merely partisan Republicanism." [18] The insurgents did not lag behind the regular Republicans in the expression of this partisanship.

The insurgents might have found Wilson's partisan methods more bearable had it not been that the Democratic President was styling his program "progressive." They deeply re-

---

12 Bristow to William Allen White, June 19, 1913, Bristow Papers.

13 Clapp to Col. E. A. Van Valkenburg, May 6, 1914, Moses E. Clapp Papers, Minnesota Historical Society, St. Paul, Minnesota.

14 Bristow to Arthur Capper, Oct. 6, 1913, Bristow Papers.

15 William E. Borah to James E. Babb, July 14, 1914, William E. Borah Papers, Library of Congress.

16 New York *Times,* April 12, 1913; *ibid.,* May 14, 1913; *ibid.,* May 28, 1913.

17 New York *Times,* July 6, 1913; *ibid.,* August 8, 1913.

18 The *New Republic,* I, No. 1, Nov. 7, 1914.

sented Wilson's decision to deny them any significant role in the formation of reform legislation. "It was the Progressive Republicans in Congress," La Follette editorialized after Wilson's victory, "who forced the issues and blazed the trails. Flanked on one side by a reactionary Democratic House machine and on the other by a Senate still in the clutches of System Republicanism, they held aloft steadfastly the Banner of Progress." [19] And then, after playing a major role in the defeat of the old system, to see the banner snatched from their grasp by up-start, wind-jamming Democrats! It was hard medicine for a group which was inclined to believe that it was the only truly progressive force in national politics. There was truth in the jibe of a Democratic Senator after one of Cummins's attacks on the caucus system when he observed that "the Senator seems to be annoyed that he was not invited into this Democratic caucus." [20]

By excluding the insurgent Republicans from a meaningful role in the enactment of the "New Freedom," Wilson all but ruled out the possibility of a bipartisan progressive coalition in Congress and in national politics. Alienated from the outset, the progressive Republicans scrutinized Wilson's programs with unfriendly eyes; and when any question arose as to the progressiveness or effectiveness of an administration bill, they were disinclined to give it the benefit of the doubt. On few occasions did they have the sense that they were joining the Democrats to enact a program of reform. Rather they seemed to feel that they were competing with Wilson for the label of "progressive." Throughout his administration they made it a primary concern to prove to the public that Wilson and the Democrats were not true progressives and that the real answer to the country's problems lay in the hands of *Republican* progressives.

Even without Wilson's partisanship as a lever, the progressive Republicans might well have remained unmoved by any Democratic overtures in 1913, so deeply were they committed

---

[19] *La Follette's Weekly*, IV, No. 45, Nov. 9, 1912.
[20] *Cong. Record*, 63 Cong., 1 Session, Sept. 9, 1913, p. 4559.

to the traditional party allegiances. Indeed, a deep-seated distrust of the Democratic party was a fundamental characteristic of their thinking. Though some progressive Republicans thought at the outset that Wilson himself might be a good man, they believed that the "southern Bourbons" and Tammany-type machine politicians with whom he would have to work were as bad, if not worse, than the Republican standpatters. The leadership of Bryan and Wilson, wrote William Allen White in November 1913, was "a temporary aberration." The Democratic party "must be historically and constitutionally the conservative party of this nation." He would sooner be a Prohibitionist or a Socialist than a Democrat, White added, "so long as it [the Democratic party] is fettered by the ideas of states rights and free trade." [21] Committed to these oboslete doctrines and dominated by "the same kind of politician that controlled the Chicago convention," as Bristow put it, how could the Democratic party be expected to stay on a progressive course? [22]

The progressive Republicans generally assumed that it would not, and they confidently awaited the day when the Democratic majorities in Congress would break up into the warring factions that had characterized the party before the Wilson era. Though Wilson seemed to be making a favorable impression, Miles Poindexter admitted in March 1913, the administration would have great difficulty preventing the "reactionary element either from controlling absolutely important measures and policies or else from so modifying them as to destroy the confidence of the people in the administration." [23] By August Poindexter thought the administration was still doing some good things but that its opponents could afford to wait for the errors which would inevitably come "in view of certain well-known fundamental doctrines to which it [the Democratic party] has committed itself." [24] William Allen

---

[21] White to Carl W. Moore, Nov. 25, 1913, White Papers.
[22] Bristow to R. C. Lappin, July 12, 1912, Bristow Papers.
[23] Poindexter to A. W. Doland, March 26, 1913, Poindexter Papers.
[24] Poindexter to T. Claude Bennett, August 9, 1913, *ibid.*

White wrote in October that he hadn't picked up a paper for six months "that I did not expect to see the beginning of the break" in Democratic unity.[25] Bristow thought the collapse would come from a rebellion of progressive Democrats and believed he saw "symptoms of rebellion" in June 1913. Only "the cohesive force of public patronage" was holding the Democrats together, he asserted.[26] Convictions such as these reinforced the inclination of the insurgents to hold to their traditional party alignment.

The reaction of the progressive Republicans to the Underwood tariff bill demonstrated the extent of their alienation from the Wilson administration and how far they were prepared to go to find positions that were Republican as well as progressive. Though the insurgents had made downward revision of the tariff one of their principal goals, they had few words in praise of Wilson's efforts to achieve this end through the Underwood-Simmons bill. In the House the progressive Republicans were solidly against the bill, and of the old Senate insurgents, only La Follette and Poindexter voted for it.[27]

Their principal objection to the Democratic measure was that it placed on the free list certain staple products of the agricultural midwest — mainly cattle and grain. The bill, Senator Cummins complained, "grievously discriminates against the West in favor of the East — that is to say in favor of the manufacturer against the farmer." [28] It was "especially discriminatory against the northern and western farmer," Bristow argued, since most of the southern products like cotton and tobacco were noncompetitive crops and would not be affected by low tariffs.[29] La Follette and Poindexter, though they chose to vote for the bill, agreed with the other insurgents that the agricultural schedule was a severe defect.[30]

---

[25] White to Homer Hock, Oct. 21, 1913, White Papers.
[26] Bristow to J. R. Harrison, June 16, 1913, Bristow Papers.
[27] New York *Times,* May 9, 1913; *ibid.,* Sept. 10, 1913.
[28] *Cong. Record,* 63 Cong., 1 Session, July 19, 1913, pp. 2554–2555.
[29] *Ibid.,* Oct. 2, 1913, p. 5312.
[30] New York *Times,* Sept. 10, 1913; Poindexter to E. K. Brown, Sept. 11, 1913, Poindexter Papers.

But the insurgents did not confine their opposition to the agricultural schedule of the tariff bill. Rather they condemned the whole measure and played a leading role in the Republican effort to discredit it. After Furnifold Simmons, Chairman of the Senate Finance committee, had opened the debate on the tariff, it was Albert Cummins who delivered the first opposition speech. In the ensuing debate the other insurgents all spoke on the bill, and in nearly every case they condemned it in no uncertain terms. They attacked its alleged discrimination against western farmers. They condemned the role of President Wilson and the Democratic caucus in the passage of the measure. They declared that it invited "the perils of free trade" and would bring about an industrial depression.[31] They condemned its inconsistencies.[32] They argued that "its discrimination in favor of localities and certain special interests" was "worse than that of the Payne-Aldrich tariff." [33]

Their position on the bill cannot be attributed to strong pressure from constituents. If anything, they took their stand in spite of popular opinion in their home states. Even Bristow, one of the most anti-Wilson progressives, admitted that the tariff bill had created a "favorable impression." [34] Senator Clapp noted that "the bill is received with a good deal of favor even by very many farmers," and that "men who were very bitter towards the Canadian [reciprocity] bill, . . . are disposed to give this a trial and await results." [35] Independent progressives like Colonel Nelson of the Kansas City *Star* commended the Democrats on the Underwood bill and attacked the Republican insurgents for voting against it.[36]

---

[31] *Cong. Record,* 63 Cong., 1 Session, July 19, 1913, pp. 2554–2555; Moses E. Clapp to Albert Beveridge, July 19, 1913, Beveridge Papers; New York *Times,* June 29, 1913.

[32] See, for instance, Bristow's speech on the tariff, *Cong. Record,* 63 Cong., 1 Session, Oct. 2, 1913, p. 5312; and Gronna's, *ibid.,* July 31, 1913, p. 2960.

[33] *Ibid.,* Oct. 2, 1913, p. 5312.

[34] Bristow to J. R. Harrison, April 12, 1913, Bristow Papers.

[35] Clapp to Beveridge, Sept. 16, 1913, Beveridge Papers.

[36] W. R. Nelson to Theodore Roosevelt, July 28, 1913, copy in the Beveridge Papers.

For a group that had built its reputation on opposition to the existing tariff system, there were obvious dangers in the policy of opposing the Underwood bill. Bristow admitted that it pained him to find himself lined up on the tariff issue with "Smoot and Penrose and the old gang that we have fought from the beginning." [37] Senator Kenyon felt called upon to make a public explanation of his vote against the bill. "I find myself in an embarrassing position as to this bill. I have advocated for many years revision of the tariff downwards; am anxious to vote for many schedules of this bill; am especially anxious to vote for the income tax feature. I do not want to cast a vote that might in any way be an approval of the Payne-Aldrich Act." [38]

But a vote against the Underwood tariff was a vote to retain the Payne-Aldrich schedules. La Follette and Poindexter based their votes in favor of the bill on just this fact.[39] There could be no possible objection to the progressives pointing out the flaws in the bill and trying to get it perfected, wrote Colonel Nelson. But ". . . in the eyes of the country there are just two alternatives open — the existing law and the Wilson-Underwood bill. People are not overexacting about legislation. They recognize that no law is perfect. But they do believe that the pending bill with its heavy reductions is an infinitely better square deal measure than the Payne-Aldrich law." [40] If the insurgents did not vote for the Underwood tariff on the final roll call, Nelson wrote, they would have grave difficulty in explaining their position to their constituents.

As Kenyon's statement makes clear, the insurgents were not unaware of the difficulties of their position, and they did their best to draw lines between themselves and the Republican Old Guard. At a meeting held in Senator La Follette's office, for instance, eleven insurgent Senators resolved that they would not follow the lead of the conservative Republicans but would

[37] Bristow to Joseph M. Dixon, May 28, 1913, *ibid.*

[38] *Cong. Record,* 63 Cong., 1 Session, August 9, 1913, p. 3219.

[39] *La Follette's Weekly,* V, No. 38, Sept. 20, 1913; Poindexter to E. K. Brown, Sept. 11, 1913, Poindexter Papers.

[40] Nelson to Roosevelt, June 27, 1913, copy in the Bristow Papers.

chart their own course, supporting some sections of the bill and opposing others.[41] In his opening attack on the Underwood-Simmons bill, Cummins was careful to condemn the Republican Old Guard as well as the Democrats. Using the analogy of Scylla and Charybdis, Cummins declared that only the progressive Republicans offered a safe passageway between these two extremes, and they would chart it in 1913 as they had done in 1909.[42]

On one important section of the tariff bill the insurgents did succeed in establishing the kind of independent progressive-Republican position they were aiming for. This was their successful effort to steepen the graduation of the income tax provision so as to make the tax burden bear more heavily on the upper income brackets. The original House version of the bill had provided for a rate of one percent on incomes over $2000, two percent on those between $50,000 and $100,000, and three percent on all incomes higher than $100,000. On August 26 Borah moved the first of a series of progressive Republican amendments providing for higher, more steeply graduated rates.[43] The next day Bristow and La Follette offered similar amendments calling for considerably higher rates than those Borah had proposed.[44] Bristow's amendment provided for a rate of one percent on the first $1000 income, rising by percentage points at every $1000 of income to a maximum of ten percent on incomes over $100,000. On the following day Bristow introduced a second amendment cutting his original rates in half in a bid for wider support, and the Progressive party's Senator, Miles Poindexter, called for a rate of twenty percent on incomes over $1,000,000.[45] Finally, on

---

[41] They were Cummins and Kenyon of Iowa, Bristow of Kansas, Borah of Idaho, Crawford and Sterling of South Dakota, Clapp of Minnesota, Gronna of North Dakota, Works of California, Norris of Nebraska, and La Follette of Wisconsin. *La Follette's Weekly,* V, No. 32, August 9, 1913; La Follette, *La Follette,* p. 476.

[42] *Cong. Record,* 63 Cong., 1 Session, July 19, 1913, pp. 2554–2555.

[43] *Ibid.,* August 26, 1913, p. 3771.

[44] *Ibid.,* August 27, 1913, p. 3805; *ibid.,* p. 3819.

[45] *Ibid.,* August 28, 1913, p. 3831; *ibid.,* p. 3835.

September 8, George Norris introduced an inheritance tax proposal providing for a levy of one percent on inheritances over $50,000, ten percent on those over $1,000,000, and seventy-five percent on inheritances of more than $50,000,000.[46]

These income tax proposals provided the insurgents with a clearly progressive issue on which they could attack the Democrats without the embarrassment of enthusiastic standpat support. The amendments were turned down by the Democratic majority, only Vardaman of Mississippi breaking the caucus rule to vote for La Follette's amendment.[47] Some standpat support came for Bristow's second weaker amendment,[48] but on the other divisions the insurgent amendments attracted only 12 to 17 votes — those of the insurgents themselves and a few other middle-road western Republicans like Jones of Washington and Sherman of Illinois.[49] Thus the movement for a stiffer income tax was clearly labelled as "progressive Republican."

The insurgents had extra reason to be satisfied with their efforts on the income tax provisions when their pressure led to a revolt in the Democratic caucus and the acceptance by the party leadership of a compromise amendment which went some of the way towards meeting the insurgents' demands.[50] This was like a return to the grand old days of the Taft administration when the insurgents had been able to use their pivotal position in the Congress to make vital changes in important legislation. The temporary split in the Democratic ranks had put the insurgents in this key position once again, and it enabled them to win a significant victory. Indeed, the institution of a federal income tax has been seen as one of the most important accomplishments of the whole "progressive era."

But from the standpoint of 1913, it was the Underwood tariff itself which was the important question, and the insur-

[46] *Ibid.*, Sept. 8, 1913, p. 4422.
[47] *Ibid.*, August 28, 1913, p. 3830.
[48] *Ibid.*, p. 3834.
[49] *Ibid.*, August 27, 1913, pp. 3818, 3830.
[50] *Ibid.*, Sept. 6, 1913, p. 4379.

gents were forced in the end to decide simply for or against the Democratic measure. Despite the inclusion in the bill of the income tax provisions that they had fought for, they voted to retain the Payne-Aldrich schedules, which they had attacked so vigorously only four years earlier. Clearly the majority of the insurgents were prepared to make few concessions to the Democratic brand of progressive reform in 1913. As far as possible they had attempted to find positions that were "progressive" as well as anti-Democratic, but where this was not possible they rejected Wilson's measure and embraced the high-tariff schedules of Nelson Aldrich.

# chapter seven

# The Reorganization Movement

The great majority of the insurgent Republicans chose to stay with the Republican party in 1912 and 1913 despite the establishment of the Progressive party and the election of a Democratic progressive to the presidency, but their decision was based chiefly on the negative consideration that the Democratic and Progressive parties did not offer viable alternatives. They were far from being overconfident about their prospects in the Republican party. Bristow could see no hope for the Republican party in the future. "The same old gang of reactionary politicians are in control and they are going to keep control," he wrote in February 1913. "I am assuming an independent attitude." [1]

Bristow was not the only insurgent to feel, early in 1913, that the only course of action that remained open was the adoption of a purely independent role in national politics. Such a posture particularly suited the political style of a man like La Follette, who had never found it easy to work with large political groups other than those he dominated. And the idea of fighting each issue on its own merits, irrespective of "political considerations" had a general appeal to men like the insurgents, who saw themselves as crusading reformers.

But for the majority of the insurgents, most of the time independence alone was an insufficient answer to their problem. In the Taft years their movement had moved from one victory

---

[1] Bristow to H. I. Maxwell, Feb. 11, 1913, Bristow Papers.

to another, or so it seemed. In 1912 the insurgents had come extraordinarily close to wresting control of the party from the hands of the conservatives. To ask the progressives to accept their defeat of that year as a final and irrevocable verdict was to ask too much. Surely, they thought, there must still be a way of advancing the progressive cause within the Republican party.

There were some grounds for hope. Few believed in 1913 that Wilson would be able to hold the Democrats together and keep his party on a progressive tack. The Republican stand-patters had been discredited by the events of 1912. Most ordinary Republican voters, the insurgents argued, were basically progressives; and as more states introduced direct primary elections, the party leadership would come to reflect the views of the rank and file as it had not done hitherto. The third party would not endure, and as it crumbled the insurgents calculated that they would get the support of the disillusioned Bull Moosers before any other faction in the two major parties. "If we can get the progressive forces back into line," Borah argued, "we can control the party and dominate its organization and its policy." [2]

But in the meantime, what relationship were the insurgents to maintain with the Old Guard of the party? After all that had happened during the four previous years, it could scarcely be a warm one. "There can be no harmony politically," Bristow warned, "between Penrose, Barnes, Murray Crane, and such type of Republicans, and La Follette, Clapp, Lenroot, Norris and myself. We do not stand for the same things and can not agree on political policies because we hold directly opposite views on most current questions." [3] Though he did not intend to "personally quarrel with individuals who believe in the old way of doing business," Borah wrote, there could be no compromises on questions of policy. [4] All the insurgents agreed that they must maintain their own separate identity within the Republican party.

---

[2] Borah to O. C. Moore, March 13, 1914, Borah Papers.
[3] Bristow to Rodney A. Elward, Dec. 4, 1912, Bristow Papers.
[4] Borah to O. C. Moore, March 13, 1914, Borah Papers.

However, with Wilson in the White House, the insurgents were notably less inclined to indulge in the savage attacks on the Republican Old Guard which had typified their rhetoric in the Taft years. Perhaps they were conscious of the fact that the Democrats were the main beneficiaries of such attacks, and for that reason preferred to concentrate their fire on Wilson. Certainly they were very sensitive to the charge of the Bull Moosers that there was no hope for progressivism inside a party controlled by conservatives. Rather than harping on the iniquities of the Republican regulars, they preferred to emphasize the progressivism of the "rank-and-file Republican" and the progressive tradition of the party back as far as Lincoln. Borah asserted that he would not remain a Republican if he did not believe that 95 percent of the Republican voters were progressives.[5] "How absurd it would be," Cummins argued, "for the clean, pure, stockholders of a bank with fifty years of honest business and accumulated good will behind it to dissolve, simply because a president, or a cashier had been found wanting in ability or integrity?"[6] The conservatism of the party leadership was not denied, but it was played down as a sort of temporary aberration.

On the positive side, the insurgent Republicans set out in the early years of the Wilson administration to convince the public that the Republican party was still an acceptable vehicle for progressive reform. This some hoped to do through a movement to "reorganize" the party. Senator Borah was one of the leading advocates of this strategy, and the subject was, according to his biographer, his chief interest between 1912 and 1916.[7] Throughout these years Borah was continuously making speeches on this theme, which he generally coupled with vigorous attacks on the Progressive party and that "notorious thief," George Perkins, with his "gigantic scheme to

---

[5] New York *Times,* Dec. 17, 1913.
[6] Speech before the Hamilton Club by A. B. Cummins, April 9, 1914, Albert B. Cummins Papers, Iowa State Department of History and Archives, Des Moines, Iowa.
[7] Johnson, *Borah,* p. 161.

protect the status quo." [8] But by reorganization Borah meant nothing more specific than an effort to remold the Republican party in a progressive image, and his speeches were largely ends in themselves — efforts to convince the public, and perhaps himself, that such a thing as a party both Republican and progressive was possible.

Other progressive Republicans were skeptical of the whole idea. A committee to reorganize the Republican party, Bristow told a group of insurgents in December 1912, would have to include the following names to have any chance of success: Theodore Roosevelt, Joseph G. Cannon, Robert M. La Follette, Hiram Johnson, Albert B. Cummins, Henry Cabot Lodge, Moses E. Clapp, and Elihu Root. "When I submitted the list," Bristow recounted, "everybody smiled." [9] Obviously the progressive and conservative wings of the party could never agree on a reorganization plan if it involved agreement between them on the major political issues of the day.

Albert Cummins, however, believed that a reorganization plan that would help restore the tarnished party image could be successful if it was limited to a program of specific changes in the party machinery. There was nothing basically wrong with the Republican party, Cummins argued. If the voters had had their way, the party would have nominated a progressive in 1912. But the indefensible proceedings at the Republican convention of that year had prevented the nomination of the people's choice and caused many Republicans to bolt their party in protest. It was therefore necessary, Cummins said, to erase a blot on the history of the party and make sure that such a thing could never happen again by reorganizing the party machinery and changing the rules of the convention.

The most important change urged by Cummins was an alteration of the composition of the National Convention to make it reflect real Republican strength. Under the existing

---

[8] Borah to C. E. Wright, March 31, 1914, Borah Papers; Borah to O. C. Moore, March 13, 1914, *ibid.*

[9] Bristow to Arthur Capper, Dec. 8, 1912, Bristow Papers.

rules the southern states were represented in the convention according to their population though there were few Republican voters in these states. Obviously enough the convention did not represent real Republican strength under these rules, and the southern delegations could usually be controlled by a President with patronage to dispense. Thus in 1912 the southern delegations had been controlled by Taft, and they were a major element in his victory. What was required was a reallocation of convention delegates according to the distribution of Republicans rather than total population.

Cummins also advocated a change in the method of choosing between contested delegations to the convention. It was not reasonable, he argued, to expect the Republican National Committee, which decided such contests under the existing system, to display judicial impartiality in the "stress and storm of political campaigns." "In the very nature of things its members become advocates of the nomination of one candidate or another." The authority of the committee to make up the temporary roll of delegates to the convention should be abolished and replaced with some more equitable system.[10]

Cummins reasoned that a reorganization plan such as this, which avoided substantive questions of policy and concentrated on the revamping of the party machinery, might well be acceptable to all factions of the party. "We cannot of course ask the men who are known as reactionaries to abandon their views upon public questions," he conceded, "nor can there be any agreement defining the path that the party is to pursue." [11] But the conservatives might well accept a more limited plan for reorganizing the party apparatus. They had nothing to lose in the immediate future by agreeing to changes in the convention rules, and they would surely hesitate to rebuff the insurgents on this issue if they thought that by doing so they would discourage Bull Moosers from re-entering the party.

---

[10] Albert B. Cummins, "The Reorganization of the Republican Party," *Saturday Evening Post,* CLXXXVI, No. 20, Nov. 15, 1913, p. 3.

[11] Cummins to Herbert Hadley, Nov. 13, 1912, copy in Crawford Papers.

A successful reorganization of the party machinery would help the insurgents by improving the image of the Republican party as a whole, but Cummins obviously intended to harness his reorganization proposals even more directly to the cause of Republican progressivism. By uniting the insurgents behind the plan he hoped to show that the progressives were still an active, vigorous force inside the Republican party. He hoped the success of the movement would bring the insurgents the kind of prestige they had won from the great intraparty battles of the Taft years. Such a victory would speed the movement of the Bull Moosers back to the G.O.P., a movement which would strengthen the progressive wing of the party still further. The ultimate goal, of course, was the nomination of a progressive as the Republican presidential nominee in 1916 — preferably the nomination of A. B. Cummins himself.

The smoke from the battles of the 1912 election campaign had scarcely cleared before Cummins launched his reorganization drive with a letter to all the prominent progressive Republicans who had not bolted the party. In it he put forward the idea that the insurgents should unite on the issue of reorganizing the party's machinery and called a meeting in Washington for December 1912.[12] This meeting, according to Bristow, turned out to be a "complete fiasco," partly because Cummins's father was taken ill in the midst of the proceedings and he had to leave the conference immediately.[13]

But the movement gathered steam in 1913 as it became increasingly clear that the insurgents were not going to support Wilson or join the Bull Moose party. On May 10 a much publicized conference of progressive Republicans opened in Chicago to launch the reorganization movement. Attending were Senators Cummins, Borah, Bristow, Kenyon, Crawford, Norris, Gronna, Sherman, and Clapp, ex-Governor Hadley, several Congressmen, and a number of others. It was not an attempt to amalgamate the Republican and Progressive parties, Cummins announced, but a meeting of Republicans

---

[12] *Ibid.*
[13] Bristow to Arthur Capper, Dec. 8, 1912, Bristow Papers.

alone.[14] The main purpose of this meeting, it is apparent, was not so much consultation as publicity, and the conferees held a public meeting at which they orated on the need for reorganizing the Republican party along the lines that Cummins had proposed. "It was party methods and not party principles that caused estrangements between parts of the party last summer," Herbert Hadley declared. Hadley called for three changes in the organization of the party: first, the cutting down of southern representation at the national convention; second, the settlement of contests between delegates in the states rather than by the national committee; and third, the holding of direct primaries in every state to choose delegates to the convention.[15]

The progressives at Chicago agreed that these changes in the party's organization could be best effected at a special party convention preferably to be held in the fall. They authorized the chairman of the conference, Senator Lawrence Y. Sherman of Illinois, to appoint a committee to draft a statement for the national committee and the public, calling for such a convention.[16] Altogether, the Chicago meeting was a great success for the Republican insurgents, as it earned them much favorable publicity in the national press. The only flaw in the proceedings was the conspicuous absence of Senator La Follette from the conference. Though Cummins stated his belief that the Wisconsin Senator was in sympathy with the purposes of the gathering, La Follette himself, typically at odds with the prevailing political trends, did not confirm the Cummins statement.[17]

Following the Chicago conference there developed in all quarters a general conviction that a special Republican national convention would indeed be held and that the party rules would be changed somewhat on the lines that the insurgents had proposed. The New York *Times* reported immediately after the conference that there was little doubt that the

[14] New York *Times,* May 11, 1913.

[15] *Ibid.,* May 13, 1913.

[16] New York *Tribune,* May 13, 1913.

[17] *Ibid.,* May 6, 1913; New York *Times,* May 11, 1913.

Taft regulars would go along with the conference idea.[18] Progressive party leaders were deeply concerned at the apparent success of the reorganization movement and did their best to discredit it. O. K. Davis, secretary of the Progressive national committee, warned Bull Moosers that the Chicago conferees were not the leaders of their party and would receive no consideration from them.[19] Congressman Hinebaugh declared that the Chicago gathering only went to show that two antagonistic, irresponsible elements were still fighting over control of the Republican party. "Every intelligent man knows," he said, "that if . . . a convention is called, it will be called by the national committee which is in absolute control of the conservative element of the party. Does anyone believe that these men will call a convention and not put themselves in control of the convention?" [20] The fact that the Bull Moosers were worried by the reorganization movement can only have encouraged the insurgents. By December 1913 it seemed that Cummins and his followers had scored a great success. They had won much favorable publicity (especially Cummins himself), the standpatters seemed compliant, and the Bull Moosers were worried. The day before the Republican national committee was to meet to discuss the convention plan on December 16, the New York *Tribune* reported that the committee was practically agreed on the convention plan.[21] A few days before it had been unanimously endorsed by the Republican congressional committee.[22]

However, when the Republican national committee met informally at a dinner given by chairman Hilles on December 15, it accepted the reorganization plan with a twist. Instead of a convention, the committee decided to make the necessary changes itself and submit its proposals to the approval of the Republican state conventions. A subcommittee of five, includ-

---

[18] *Ibid.,* May 14, 1913.
[19] *Ibid.;* for the private opinions of the Bull Moosers concerning the reorganization movement, see pp. 74–75 above.
[20] New York *Tribune,* May 14, 1913.
[21] *Ibid.,* Dec. 15, 1913.
[22] New York *Times,* Dec. 13, 1913.

ing Borah and Hadley, was set up to draft two resolutions to be presented at the formal sessions the next day.[23] When it met in formal session, the committee adopted unanimously two resolutions, one reducing the number of delegates to the national convention from the south, and the other giving full recognition to the principle of the primary election in the selection of delegates to the national convention.[24]

Various reasons were given for setting aside the convention plan. Borah said that he was opposed to it because the delegates to a convention would be picked by politicians and not by the people and would not therefore be representative. The more usual reason given was that a convention would only lead to renewed outbreaks of the violent quarreling between the sections of the party which had fought so bitterly in 1912.[25] But Cummins had already announced that he had "no intention of demanding that a national convention should adopt a general party platform," and went no further than urging that the convention deal with "the proposed changes in delegate representation and party rules." [26] With matters of policy excluded and a general consensus already established on the need for revising the party machinery, why should there be any more dissension at the convention than there was at the committee meeting itself?

The truth was that the conservative majority on the national committee was opposed to the convention plan for precisely the same reasons that the insurgents wanted it. As Cummins said, the convention would have been a major political event and would have impressed the public more than any act of the national committee.[27] It was one thing to agree to some relatively harmless changes in the composition of the national convention and to make statements of principle about primaries. But there was no need to give Cummins and his cohorts even more glory by providing them with a special national

---

[23] *Ibid.,* Dec. 16, 1913.
[24] *Ibid.,* Dec. 17, 1913.
[25] New York *Tribune,* Dec. 17, 1913.
[26] *Ibid.,* Sept. 16, 1913.
[27] New York *Times,* Dec. 17, 1913.

convention as a forum. There was even the possibility, as the Massachusetts Republican boss, Murray Crane, suggested to Elihu Root, "that the so-called 'progressives,' who met at Chicago recently, will endeavor to and may control that convention." [28]

In public, Cummins and the other insurgents declared themselves satisfied with the committee's action, though Cummins said he was sorry the convention plan had not been proceeded with.[29] The new rules, Bristow wrote to a constituent, "made it absolutely impossible for a machine to control the convention." [30] Borah declared that "the machinery of the party is now in the hands of the voter." [31] But privately, Cummins admitted that the action of the committee had been a setback. He was "grievously disappointed" and mystified by Borah's attitude at the meeting, though he admitted that Borah had been against the convention idea at the Chicago meeting.[32]

The Bull Moosers, on the other hand, were jubilant at the rebuff the national committee had handed the insurgents. It "strengthens enormously your position as an out-and-out anti-compromise Progressive," Mark Sullivan wrote to Beveridge. "Amalgamation talk reached the greatest height that it will ever reach just previous to the meeting of the National Committee; from now on it will ebb." [33] The committee had made an even greater blunder than it had made in 1912, Beveridge thought, and he could not understand why Cummins did not see the light and join the Progressive party.[34]

Instead of forcing Cummins and his associates out of the Republican into the Progressive party, the action of the national committee underlined their commitment to the G.O.P.

---

[28] Murray Crane to Elihu Root, May 21, 1913, Root Papers.

[29] New York *Times,* Dec. 17, 1913.

[30] Bristow to H. M. Laing, Feb. 4, 1914, Bristow Papers.

[31] Quoted in Marion C. McKenna, *Borah* (Ann Arbor, Mich., 1961), p. 135.

[32] Cummins to Beveridge, Jan. 14, 1914, Beveridge Papers.

[33] Sullivan to Beveridge, Dec. 22, 1913, *ibid.*

[34] Beveridge to Sullivan, Dec. 27, 1913, *ibid.*; Beveridge to Poindexter, Dec. 27, 1913, *ibid.*

While privately he had felt "deeply disappointed," Cummins had felt obliged to accept the committee's decision with good grace and even to declare himself largely satisfied. Nowhere is the weakness of the progressive Republican movement after 1912 made more clear.

The reorganization strategy pushed by Cummins, Hadley, and others had been successful up to a point. Cummins had managed to unite most of the insurgents behind his leadership, and the conservatives had accepted the substance of his demands. But the action of the national committee in December and the progressives' reaction to it showed that the ability of the insurgents to influence the party as a whole depended, as before, entirely on the sufferance of the Old Guard. The conservative majority might deem it expedient to make concessions to the progressive wing of the party from time to time; but when it made up its mind to draw the line and insist on conservative policies, there was precious little that the insurgents could do about it. The progressives hoped that the conservatives would feel impelled to make some concession in order to attract the votes of the Bull Moosers. But what if the standpatters chose to stick to a conservative line and wait for the development of an anti-Wilson reaction?

In fact, something like this did seem to be happening after the first few months of the Wilson administration. The Republican regulars concentrated on the tariff issue, predicting industrial depression as a result of the Underwood tariff measure. When a minor depression did develop late in 1913, the standpatters became even more confident that the Democrats could be defeated on traditional issues without any substantial concessions to the progressive point of view. Deprived of any substantial leverage on the conservative leadership of the party, the progressive Republicans retained very little national influence or national power, remaining a vocal but weak minority in a minority party.

# chapter eight

# The Negative Approach

A year after Woodrow Wilson's inauguration, the Bull Moose Senator, Miles Poindexter of Washington, wrote an appraisal of the Democratic administration for *Harper's Weekly*. "I think any unprejudiced and free-minded person of whatever party," Poindexter wrote, "must admit that President Wilson, during the short time he has been in office, has not only a wonderful record of accomplishments, but that he has made a good impression upon the public." [1] Most of the insurgents, however, were not unprejudiced and free-minded when it came to the Wilson administration. They were highly critical of Wilson's "accomplishments," and his undoubted popularity only stirred them on to greater efforts in their campaign to prove that Wilson was not a genuine progressive. Individually some of them supported Wilson from time to time, particularly La Follette. But in general the insurgents opposed the President's legislative program, always on the ground that his proposals were reactionary or, at any rate, not progressive enough. Only one major administration bill escaped severe criticism by the insurgent bloc in the Senate and attracted their votes as a group.

Wilson followed his tariff revision bill with a proposal to reform the national system of banking and currency. In retrospect the measure that emerged, the Federal Reserve Act of 1913, appears as one of the most significant achievements of

---

[1] *Harper's Weekly*, LVIII, No. 20851, March 7, 1914.

the Wilson administration and of the whole progressive era. But at the time of its enactment, some of the most bitter attacks on the Federal Reserve bill came from the progressive wing of the Republican party.

Like the Underwood tariff, the Federal Reserve bill was pushed through Congress as a purely partisan measure, and the important decisions as to its general shape and particular provisions were fought out within the Democratic party. The progressive Republicans attacked this aspect of the bill with the same vigor that they had shown in denouncing the partisan character of the Underwood tariff. Norris believed that the Democratic leadership was not only attempting to force its own followers into line on the bill but was trying "to put it [the bill] in such shape as to drive away any votes except Democratic votes," and he believed that the President was chiefly to blame for this policy.[2]

In the House, the Democratic leadership had the bill firmly in hand, and debate on the floor lasted only a few days. The progressive Republicans there developed no distinctive stand on the measure, though some of them raised various objections to it, including of course the obnoxious caucus methods the Democrats had employed to push the bill through.[3] On the final vote some of the insurgents voted for it and some against.[4]

---

[2] Norris to R. R. Reed, Feb. 9, 1914, Norris Papers.

[3] New York *Times*, Sept. 11, 1913; *ibid.*, Sept. 14, 1913.

[4] Identifying the insurgents among the House Republicans has been

The Wisconsin representatives were solidly for the bill, but it won little support among the delegations from the other insurgent states.

In the Senate, the Federal Reserve bill ran into severe difficulties, owing to the obstruction of three antiadministration Democrats on the Senate Banking and Currency committee.[5] With the three Democrats Hitchcock, O'Gorman, and Reed siding with the Republican minority, the committee remained deadlocked on the bill for several weeks; and during the long delay the opposition forces developed a more systematic criticism of the bill than had emerged from the House debates. In mid-October, when it seemed that Wilson had won over two of the insurgent Democrats and possibly some of the Republicans on the committee, the opposition crystallized once more around a rival bill, drawn up by Senator Hitchcock, that was based upon a plan presented to the committee by Frank A. Vanderlip of the National City Bank of New York.[6]

One of the most fervent critics of the administration's banking and currency proposals and a warm advocate of the Hitchcock bill was Senator Joseph Bristow, who was a member of the Banking and Currency committee. Most of the other insurgents in the Senate followed his lead. The chief objection of the insurgent Republicans to the administration's bill was that the member banks would own the stock and appoint the di-

---

a difficult task for obvious reasons. Being less prominent than the Senators, the views and political affiliations of Congressmen are not so well publicized. I have drawn up a tentative list of 44 insurgent Republicans in the Sixty-second Congress (1911–1912) drawn from information in *La Follette's Weekly,* II, No. 46, Nov. 19, 1910; the New York *Times,* August 4, 1911; Lynn Haines, *Law Making in America, the Story of the 1911–1912 Session of the Sixty-Second Congress* (Bethesda, Md., 1912), *passim*; and various other scattered sources. Of these 44, 29 came from the north-central area. Thirty-one of the forty-four were re-elected to the Sixty-third Congress in 1912, four of whom joined the Bull Moose organization in the House. Of the remaining twenty-seven, twelve voted for the Federal Reserve bill, eleven against it, and four abstained. New York *Times,* Sept. 19, 1913.

[5] Link, *The New Freedom,* pp. 227ff.
[6] *Ibid.*

rectors of the new regional reserve banks. La Follette characterized this as "turning the job of destroying the monster that controls capital and enslaves credit over to the bankers." [7]

Instead of a "banker's bank," Bristow advocated a "people's bank" in which the stock would be owned by the public and the directors appointed by the government.[8] To allow the banks control of the stock and directorships of the regional banks, Borah argued, gave them complete control of the currency. Such a power should belong to the government and not to private institutions. Giving it to the banks "takes from the people a sovereign right and parcels it out to those whose prime interest must be that of gain." [9] Far from destroying the "money trust," Senator Works declared, "this bill lays the foundation for one of the greatest trusts this country has ever known." [10] The currency bill, as it finally passed, was in Bristow's opinion, "the most reactionary measure that has passed Congress in twenty-five years. It fastened the power of the money trust upon the country." [11]

While the progressive wing of the Republican party was attacking the Federal Reserve bill from the left, the standpatters were busy assailing it as a dangerously radical measure. It put the government into the banking business, Lodge said, when the aim should be just the opposite.[12] It was inflationary, according to Root, and if it passed "America stands to lose all it saved when Grant vetoed the inflation bill, all we saved when Grover Cleveland abolished the silver purchase, all we saved when we elected McKinley." [13]

The Democrats were not slow to seize upon the obvious contradictions in the Republican attack. While one Republican "attempts to make out that Mr. Bryan is at the bottom of this bill, and that it is a complete surrender to his views

---

[7] *La Follette's Weekly,* VI, No. 1, Jan. 3, 1914.

[8] *Cong. Record,* 63 Cong., 2 Session, Dec. 9, 1913, p. 529.

[9] *Ibid.,* Dec. 12, 1913, pp. 762–763.

[10] *Ibid.,* Dec. 15, 1913, p. 896.

[11] Bristow to M. M. Beck, Feb. 7, 1914, Bristow Papers.

[12] Lodge to John W. Weeks, Dec. 18, 1913, Lodge Papers.

[13] *Cong. Record,* 63 Cong., 2 Session, Dec. 13, 1913, p. 835.

concerning banking and currency," a Democratic Senator pointed out, "we only an hour ago heard the Senator from Kansas [Bristow] say that we had absolutely surrendered to the trusts in this matter." [14] The Democrats were obviously delighted by the alliance of insurgent and standpat Republicans on the Federal Reserve bill. Senator Lewis of Illinois chided Bristow that "when he sought the votes of Kansas at any time successfully, he got them by crying out the names of Gallinger, Root, and Penrose, and by the names of this Mephistophelean trinity was enabled to win the approval of Kansas . . . ; I was pained to note that at the very first opportunity coming to him he was found casting his vote with these gentlemen, with these eminent Senators . . . so long . . . denounced by him as the source of all public danger." [15]

The solidarity which the Republican Senators of both factions showed on this bill certainly was remarkable in view of the fact that while one group called it reactionary and the other radical, both agreed that the Hitchcock bill was better! Arthur Link has shown how different features of the Vanderlip plan appealed to both the progressive and conservative critics of the administration: "So-called radicals like Reed and Bristow and nearly all the insurgent Republican Senators liked the thoroughgoing measure of public control that it provided. Conservatives like Hitchcock and Senator John W. Weeks of Massachusetts approved because it provided for the creation of a central bank and required national banks to subscribe only to that portion of the Reserve Bank's capital stock not taken by the public or by the government." [16] The private correspondence of the insurgents leaves no doubt that they genuinely believed what they said in public about the superiority of the Hitchcock bill over the administration plan. Nevertheless, as the New York *Times* commented, the formation of "something like a systematic criticism of the administration bill" from "such dissimilar points of view as those

14 *Ibid.,* Dec. 23, 1913, p. 1483.
15 *Ibid.,* p. 1480.
16 Link, *The New Freedom,* p. 233.

reported by the Senator from Kansas, Mr. Bristow, and the Senator from Massachusetts, Mr. Weeks," was certainly "curious." [17] Clearly the impetus behind such an alliance was as much political as ideological. Insurgents like Bristow could not afford to admit, even to themselves, that Wilson's "New Freedom" was an acceptable progressive program. On almost every major Democratic proposal during the Wilson years the same pattern emerged. Conservative Republicans condemned the measure as being dangerously radical; progressive Republicans declared it to be reactionary; then both groups joined to vote against it.

Early in 1913 Bristow had written that the two wings of the Republican party could never work together. But a year later, as his heart hardened against the New Freedom, he found the standpatters more congenial allies. "Between you and me," he wrote to William Allen White in December 1913, "these so-called 'progressive' Democrats are usually fakes when they get to Washington. I am having a fight now with the so-called 'progressive' Democrats on this currency bill, and I find them ultra-reactionary. So far as voting is concerned in the Senate now on genuine progressive measures it is just as easy to get a standpat Republican's vote as a 'progressive' Democrat's, and a good deal easier if it happens to be something upon which Mr. Wilson does not look with favor, and mark it down, Wilson is not a progressive." [18] In January 1914 Bristow confided that he could work effectively as a progressive in the Republican party. The conservative Republicans who had once derided La Follette, Cummins, and himself were now "rather eager to vote with us." On the banking and currency bill he had found his conservative colleagues willing to vote all his progressive amendments except one. ". . . the conservative Republicans out of power are growing rapidly progressive; the Democratic progressives in power are growing rapidly conservative," he declared.[19] Thus far had his hatred of Wilson carried Bristow by 1914.

---

[17] New York *Times,* Oct. 1, 1913.

[18] Bristow to White, Dec. 13, 1913, Bristow Papers.

[19] Bristow to William Palmer, Jan. 14, 1914, *ibid.*

Probably no other important progressive Republican was so sanguine about the future of progressive-conservative relationships within the Republican party as Bristow at this point, but their public attitudes to the Wilson administration were no different. The pattern established in 1913 during the debates on the Underwood tariff and the Federal Reserve bill was repeated time and time again. Throughout his first administration President Wilson came under continuous attack from the progressive Republicans for dictatorial administrative policies and reactionary legislative programs. Under Taft the insurgent Republicans had joined the Democrats to enact a number of important progressive reforms, but the legislative achievements of the Wilson years were, by and large, the work of Democrats and Democrats alone.

Only once was this pattern broken on an important issue. Led by Albert Cummins, the majority of the progressive Republicans in the Senate supported and voted for the Federal Trade Commission bill of 1914. It seems hardly coincidental that this was also the one major item of Wilson's legislative program which insurgent Republicans were allowed to help frame. In the early months of 1914 it seemed that as usual, the insurgents in the Senate were going to be excluded from the process of drafting the anti-trust bills with the probable result that they would be alienated from the administration on yet another major issue. In January it was reported that Democrats did not intend to share any of the credit which they expected to gain from the passage of the bills with the Republicans,[20] and by February a floor fight by the "radical Republicans" to sharpen the teeth of Wilson's proposed trade commission was expected.[21] In protest against the evident intention of the Democrats to exclude them from the drafting process, the two insurgents on the Interstate Commerce committee, Clapp and Cummins, refused to attend a meeting of the committee with the President or to have anything to do with the committee's work.[22] However, for reasons that are

---

[20] New York *Times,* Jan. 15, 1914.
[21] *Ibid.,* Feb. 1, 1914.
[22] *Ibid.,* Feb. 12, 1914.

not entirely clear, the Democrats soon made an about-face and contrary to their usual practice invited Senator Cummins to serve on a new subcommittee to draft the Federal Trade Commission bill.[23] The results were remarkable. Senator Cummins, the ranking minority member of the committee, emerged as one of the leading proponents of the bill when it reached the floor of the Senate; and most, but not all, of the Republican insurgents followed his lead. The bill was, as the committee chairman Senator Newlands said, a "thoroughly non-partisan" measure,[24] and its most important and controversial clause was identical with one in a bill which Senator Clapp had brought before the committee.[25]

The Federal Trade Commission bill set up an independent bipartisan commission modeled on the Interstate Commerce Commission. Its most vital and bitterly contested provision gave the commission power to investigate instances of "unfair competition," and where it found them, to issue cease and desist orders, enforceable by the federal courts. The bill, Professor Link has remarked, closely resembled "the kind of legislation that Roosevelt had proposed in 1912," [26] and Wilson's conversion to this approach to the trust problem marked the fact that the President "had accepted almost entirely the New Nationalism's solution for the regulation of business by a powerful trade commission." [27]

Some progressives in both parties interpreted the Federal Trade Commission bill in much the same way at the time and attacked it as part of a policy of regulating rather than destroying monopoly. The bill marked the time, according to Borah, "when the question of competition will be eliminated entirely, and we will simply undertake to regulate and control the combinations." [28] To try and regulate monopoly, Borah declared, was like trying to regulate a cancer in the

---

[23] Des Moines *Register,* March 13, 1914; Norris to F. A. Good, June 15, 1914, Norris Papers.
[24] New York *Times,* June 14, 1914.
[25] *Ibid.,* June 13, 1914.
[26] Link, *The New Freedom,* p. 439.
[27] Link, *Wilson and the Progressive Era,* p. 70.
[28] *Cong. Record,* 63 Cong., 2 Session, June 26, 1914, p. 1186.

human system. State socialism was preferable.[29] Senator Works charged that far from "putting big business in the hands of . . . a commission . . . , the Commission and with it the Government may fall into the hands of the powerful combinations of wealth." [30]

As previously discussed,[31] Cummins and those progressives who supported the bill did not defend it in terms of the "New Nationalism." It was not intended, Cummins said, that the commission should recognize monopoly and simply "check its ravages." Rather the commission would have the power to "prevent the monopoly from coming into existence at all." [32] It would do this by suppressing "unfair competition," which was "the deadliest enemy of independence in business." [33] Borah and his associates were hard put to refute this argument since they agreed that monopoly arose only from unfair and illegal practices, not from the nature of capitalistic competition itself. Consequently, they concentrated their attacks on the definition of "unfair competition," which they argued was so vague as to be meaningless.

When the Federal Trade Commission bill came to a vote in the Senate, Borah and Works abstained, but Cummins, La Follette, and all the other progressive Republicans either voted for it or announced that they supported it.[34] This bipartisan progressive front did not last. When the second part of Wilson's anti-trust legislative program reached the Senate in the form of the Clayton bill, the progressive Republicans were once more found in opposition to the Democratic administration. The Clayton bill outlawed a large number of business practices which were considered monopolistic or "unfair," such as tying agreements and interlocking directorates. It had passed the House overwhelmingly on June 5, 1914 with the support

29 *Ibid.*, June 29, 1914, p. 11299.
30 *Ibid.*, July 17, 1914, p. 12276.
31 See pp. 13–14 above.
32 *Cong. Record,* 63 Cong., 2 Session, July 25, 1914, p. 12733.
33 *Ibid.*, July 29, 1914, p. 12919.
34 *Ibid.*, Aug. 5, 1914, p. 13319.

of 16 Bull Moosers and 43 Republicans.[35] But before the passage of the Clayton bill in the House, Wilson had changed his views on the trust question and decided to base his antitrust program on the strong commission plan embodied in the Federal Trade Commission bill.[36] He had then lost interest in the Clayton bill and allowed the Senate Judiciary committee to take most of the teeth out of it with a series of crippling amendments.[37]

The results of this process were vigorously attacked by a Democratic Senator, James A. Reed of Missouri, and his lead was followed by some other Democrats and all the progressive Republicans in the Senate. They attacked the deletion of those sections of the bill which prohibited tying agreements and local price-cutting. They moved to restore the penal provisions of the House bill that the Senate committee had struck out. They attacked and attempted to remove the numerous modifying clauses that the Senate committee had inserted. (The committee, for instance, had made interlocking directorates within one industry illegal only where the effect would be "to substantially lessen competition," and it had made price discrimination illegal only where specific "intent thereby to destroy or wrongfully injure the business of a competitor" could be proven.) These attacks had almost no success since the Democratic majority supported the Judiciary committee's amendments and the Republican conservatives also lent their support to the committee's bill.[38]

On the final roll call, most of the progressive Republicans in the Senate voted for the Clayton bill, in the hope that the conference committee would restore some of the tougher provisions of the House version.[39] But on examining the confer-

---

[35] *La Follette's Weekly,* VI, No. 24, June 13, 1914.
[36] Link, *The New Freedom,* p. 438.
[37] *Ibid.,* pp. 442–443.
[38] For a summary of the insurgents' objections to the Clayton bill as it appeared in the Senate, see Senator Reed's speech, *Cong. Record,* 63 Cong., 2 Session, Sept. 28, 1914, p. 15818.
[39] *Ibid.,* Sept. 2, 1914, p. 14610.

ence report, they concluded that the conferees had "kept what was bad in both bills," [40] and Norris attacked it savagely as "the greatest victory of a legislative nature that has been won by the trusts and combinations within the lifetime of any man here." [41] It was clear, Bristow said, that the President "is not in favor of enacting into law the things that he advocated in the 'New Freedom,' in other words that he has surrendered his administration to the sinister influences in this Republic, and from now on there will not be and has not been for half a century an administration so abjectly subservient to the Wall Street influence as the present one." [42] Not one progressive Republican Senator voted for the conference report of the Clayton bill unless one counts Poindexter, the Bull Mooser. [43]

Since the insurgents had attacked the major parts of Wilson's "New Freedom," voting against three out of four of the major bills which made up the program, it was scarcely to be expected that they would show much more sympathy to the administration as it moved into its next, more conservative phase. [44] This conservatism was reflected mainly in the President's refusal to embark on further programs of progressive reform during 1914 and 1915, a phenomenon which did not in itself produce any direct confrontation between the President and the Republican insurgents. But the President's retreat from militant progressivism also showed itself in some of his appointments to the regulatory agencies, and the progressive Republicans were quick to attack these when they came up for confirmation in the Senate. In late January 1914 the President announced the appointment of Winthrop M. Daniels and Henry Clay Hall to the Interstate Commerce Commission. The insurgents were outraged by these appointments, particularly that of Daniels, whom they believed had shown a marked pro-railroad bias during his service as a

---

[40] *Ibid.*, Oct. 2, 1914, p. 16042.

[41] *Ibid.*, p. 16043.

[42] *Ibid.*, p. 16056.

[43] *Ibid.*, Oct. 5, 1914, p. 16170.

[44] Link, *Wilson and the Progressive Era*, pp. 54–80.

member of the New Jersey Public Utilities Commission.[45] In April the insurgents, led by La Follette, conducted a three day fight against the confirmation of Daniels and created "one of the most sensational and dramatic scenes that was ever witnessed in the Senate," according to the Des Moines *Register,* by refusing to keep secret the Senate's proceedings which were conducted behind closed doors in executive session.[46] In July and August the insurgents attacked some of Wilson's appointments to the Federal Reserve Board, particularly Paul M. Warburg, against whom Bristow delivered a four hour speech.[47]

In 1915 another issue arose, partly international in character, that put the insurgents in direct opposition to Wilson once again. This was the administration's request for an appropriation of $30 million to buy a government owned and operated shipping line, supposedly in order to meet the special needs of the nation during the World War. The Republican Old Guard, led by Elihu Root and Henry Cabot Lodge, opposed the plan partly because they suspected (correctly) that the administration intended to buy the German ships that were trapped in American ports. Such a step would be a "gross departure from the spirit if not the letter of neutrality," Lodge argued, and was further proof that "at heart he [Wilson] is friendly to the Germans." [48] They were also opposed to the idea of the Government entering the shipping business, which Lodge said would put "a complete stop" to the development of an American merchant Marine.[49]

Typically, the progressive Republicans joined the conservatives in opposition to the Ship Purchase bill, though giving entirely different reasons for doing so. What they objected to in the measure was that instead of providing for the government's direct intervention in the shipping business, it set up

---

[45] La Follette, *La Follette,* p. 489.
[46] Des Moines *Register,* April 4, 1914; New York *Times,* April 4, 1914.
[47] New York *Times,* July 10, 1914; *ibid.,* August 8, 1914.
[48] Lodge to Jacob H. Gallinger, Nov. 13, 1914, Lodge Papers.
[49] *Ibid.*

a corporation in which ownership and control would be shared by the government and private interests. He was not opposed to the government purchasing ships, Albert Cummins said, but he was totally opposed to the kind of big government-big business partnership which this bill seemed to envisage.[50] In horrified tones, Cummins drew a picture of the Secretary of the Treasury and other high government officials sitting down to discuss the business of the corporation with J. P. Morgan and other shipping magnates.[51] It was, Cummins said, "the most reactionary, indefensible, legislation which, so far as my knowledge goes, has ever appeared in Congress." [52] At one stage it seemed that Wilson had won over some of the insurgent Republican Senators whose support he needed, on this occasion, to pass the bill.[53] But though the President agreed to accept some insurgent amendments which would have made the bill acceptable to La Follette and Norris, his heavy-handed attempt to put pressure on Senator Kenyon eventually lost him the support of both Kenyon and Norris; and when the bill came up again later in the House, Norris, Kenyon, and La Follette were further alienated by a provision that would have ended the operation of the government ships after the war had ended.[54]

On occasion the insurgents in these years went to absurd lengths to prove that Wilson's policies were unprogressive. Cummins, for instance, attempted to justify his vote against the appointment of Brandeis to the Supreme Court in 1916 on the grounds of his background as a corporation lawyer and his advocacy of a "soft policy" toward the railroads before the Interstate Commerce Commission two years previously.[55] On the other hand, there was very often a solid basis for the

---

[50] Des Moines *Register,* Jan. 23, 1915.
[51] *Cong. Record,* 63 Cong. 3 Session, Feb. 8, 1915, p. 3404.
[52] *Ibid.,* Jan. 22, 1915, p. 2085.
[53] New York *Times,* Feb. 3 and 4, 1915.
[54] Arthur S. Link, *Wilson, The Struggle for Neutrality, 1914–1915* (Princeton, 1960), pp. 155–158; *Cong. Record,* 63 Cong., 3 Session, Feb. 8, 1915, p. 3254; *ibid.,* p. 3412.
[55] Sayre, *Cummins,* p. 450.

insurgents' attacks on Wilson's policies from a "progressive" standpoint. Certainly none of his policies were radical, and some of them, such as the appointments to the Federal Reserve Board, were plainly conservative.

By attacking Wilson from the left, however, the insurgent Republicans exposed themselves to the charges of hypocrisy and inconsistency. For if Wilson's fault was overconservatism, as they alleged, how could they justify their allegiance to the Republican party, the bulk of which was demonstrably more conservative than Wilson? A left-right alliance against the center might be useful as a parliamentary tactic on occasions, but it was difficult to defend from the hustings.

The Bull Moosers seized upon this fact in their attacks on the Republican party. Though they had little grass-roots strength, the Progressives were at least free from the kind of embarrassing party alignment which bothered the Republican insurgents, and they exploited this advantage for all it was worth. "If we in the Republican party with Roosevelt as its leader could not stem reactionary sentiment in the party, what hope is there for regenerating the party now?" Senator Clapp asked during his Progressive party period. "If the term 'progressive' means something other than Republican, it is illogical to split the two." [56] When the Progressive party began to disintegrate after the elections of 1914 and men like Clapp and Poindexter moved to reaffiliate themselves with the Republican party once more, they were of course in an even more embarrassing position than those who had never left the G.O.P. in the first place. But for the first two years of the Wilson administration they could afford to stand on their principles and denounce their erstwhile comrades who had deserted principles for political advantage.

The defense offered by the insurgent Republicans against such attacks as these was not very convincing. They had political reality with them, for by staying inside the Republican party they could at least maintain their strength in their home

---

[56] Article by Moses E. Clapp written for Progressive newspapers, May 23, 1914, Clapp Papers.

states. But in order to justify themselves, they were forced to resort to some rather dubious arguments, even by the standards of ordinary political debate. They condemned Wilson not merely as too moderate a reformer, but as an "ultra-conservative; not as much a progressive as Taft is," to quote Bristow.[57] The Republican party was praised for its progressive traditions and the progressiveness of its "rank-and-file."

As for the immediate problem of party division, Bristow discovered in 1914 a "spirit throughout the country among Republicans of both branches of the party to get rid of the present national incubus and then fight out our factional controversies." [58] Cummins argued that the great national questions of the day could be "more confidently trusted to the coherence of Republican thought than to the slavish obligation of a democratic caucus." Certainly "there will remain a genuine difference among Republicans as to the best legislation upon these subjects," but out of such "honest and wholesome conflict" would come, in the end, truth and justice.[59]

In fact, however, the two wings of the Republican party disagreed on almost every point except the desirability of removing the Wilson administration from power.

---

57 Bristow to W. Y. Morgan, May 23, 1914, Bristow Papers.
58 Bristow to P. W. Heath, April 13, 1914, *ibid.*
59 Draft for speech, dated only 1915, Cummins Papers.

# chapter nine

# International Issues, 1914–1916

Around the middle of Woodrow Wilson's first presidential term, the growing importance of foreign policy issues began to affect the shape of American politics. The remarkable solidarity that the Democratic party had managed to maintain through most of 1913 and 1914 started to crumble under the impact of the new international problems and Wilson's handling of them. The Bull Moosers moved steadily closer to reunion with the G.O.P. as their leader, Theodore Roosevelt, played down the domestic policies opposed by the Republican regulars and concentrated on attacking Wilson's foreign policy. Finally, the progressive Republicans became more alienated than ever from the conservative leadership of their party, as international affairs raised yet another series of issues on which the two wings of the party disagreed.

Quite apart from the progressive-conservative split in the party, the Republicans presented far from a solid front on the troublesome international issues of these years. Whether Wilson was risking war by taking a militant stand or striving for peace by avoiding one, opposition to his policies was patently full of risks. To take an unpopular stand on an issue as explosive as war and peace could well mean political suicide. Consequently the immediate reactions of Republican politicians to Wilson's crucial foreign policy decisions were often varied and hesitant.[1]

[1] See, for instance, New York *Times,* May 15, 1915; *ibid.,* April 20, 1916.

Nevertheless, certain general patterns stand out clearly enough. The Republican leaders who had guided American foreign policy in the years before 1913 — Roosevelt, Taft, Lodge, and Root — stood at the forefront of those critics of Wilson who believed that the President's foreign policies were too weak, too vacillating, too pacific.[2] On the other hand, among those who believed that Wilson's policies were too belligerent, none were more prominent than the Republican insurgents. A small minority of the progressive wing of the Republican party including William E. Borah, Thomas Sterling, and Miles Poindexter, who had rejoined the party in 1915, joined the conservatives in advocating a militant foreign policy. But the dominant sentiment among the insurgent Republicans in these years was for an isolationist, pacific approach to foreign affairs. Thus the emergence of foreign policy as a major issue in American national politics tended to widen the gap between the progressive and conservative wings of the G.O.P.

As on domestic issues, Republican differences on foreign policy were sometimes obscured by a common antipathy to Wilson and the Democratic party. Such was the case in April 1914, when the administration faced the first major crisis in its Mexican policy. The crisis was one of the President's own making. Attempting to overthrow the Mexican dictator, Victoriano Huerta, and to help establish liberal, democratic government in that country, Wilson seized upon a minor incident involving American sailors at Tampico to intervene in Mexican affairs with armed force. On April 20 he appeared before Congress and requested authority to use force in order to obtain redress for an alleged insult to the flag. The next day, while Congress was still debating the issue, Wilson ordered marines to land and seize the port of Vera Cruz in order to prevent the entry of a shipment of arms to the Huerta government. This was done the following day in an action which

---

[2] Richard Leopold, *Elihu Root and the Conservative Tradition* (Boston, 1954), p. 98.

cost the Mexicans 126 killed and 195 wounded. The American forces lost 19 dead and 71 wounded.[3]

Wilson had not been frank with the public as to what the real purpose of the intervention was. Consequently, there was considerable astonishment in the United States and elsewhere that the American government should cause blood to be spilled over such a trifling matter as a salute to the flag. In Congress the Republicans, both progressives and conservatives, were extremely critical of the administration's actions. In the Senate they united behind an amendment to the proposed resolution offered by Henry Cabot Lodge. Lodge did not argue that intervention, *per se,* was a bad idea or that "due atonement" should not be demanded for an insult to the flag, but intervention, he said, should be based on "the broadest possible grounds," namely the protection of American lives and property in Mexico. Nor should there be any implication that the United States was supporting "one murderer and cut-throat in preference to another murderer and cut-throat." [4] All the Republican insurgents in the Senate except La Follette and Bristow voted for Lodge's amendment,[5] and Bristow said that if intervention was justified at all, the Lodge amendment provided the best grounds.[6] Saluting the flag, Norris said, was "an ancient international custom of barbarism," a "foolish rule," and the incident under debate offered a good opportunity to get rid of it.[7] Republican harmony on the Vera Cruz incident was more apparent than real, however. Though the insurgents preferred Lodge's justification for war to Wilson's, most of them were strongly opposed to intervention in Mexico on any grounds at all, whereas Lodge and conservative Republicans like Albert Fall of New Mexico were advocates of strong action in Mexico to protect American interests there.

In the debates on Mexican policy that occurred during the

---

[3] Link, *Wilson and the Progressive Era,* pp. 122–123.

[4] *Cong. Record,* 63 Cong., 2 Session, April 21, 1914, p. 6966.

[5] *Ibid.,* p. 7006.

[6] *Ibid.,* p. 6997.

[7] *Ibid.,* p. 6999.

next two years, Borah was the only leading insurgent who took a strong, aggressive line on the issue. The others tended to interpret calls for intervention in Mexico as yet another plot by "the interests" to foist their economic power on an innocent group which wanted none of it. In January 1916, when the atrocities of the Mexico bandit Pancho Villa aroused widespread demands for U. S. intervention, La Follette declared in his magazine that there was no cause for intervention and that the pressure for such action came from big business with an interest in economic imperialism.[8] Albert Cummins criticized Wilson's Mexican policy, but rather than calling for intervention he attacked the administration for allowing the "constitutionalist" rebels to buy arms and supplies in the United States.[9] As a rule, the insurgents preferred to avoid the issue altogether.

It was less easy to avoid the more significant issues that arose out of America's neutrality in the World War, though there is some evidence that the insurgents would have preferred to do so. In 1915, for example, the front page editorials of La Follette's monthly magazine touched on the issues arising from the war only twice in twelve issues — this in a year when the daily newspapers all over the country were overflowing with news from the European war, and in which the United States came to the brink of war with the Central powers. *La Follette's Magazine* never mentioned the sinking of the *Lusitania* and the ensuing diplomatic crisis, though it featured a front page editorial on the tragic sinking of the steamer *Eastland* in the Chicago river on June 26. This desire to push the war issues out of sight may have reflected a fear that international involvement and war would distract the country from domestic reform, something William Allen White thought he saw happening in September 1914.[10] More certainly it reflected a simple aversion on the part of the insurgents to American involvement in the European blood bath, a sentiment that was shared by rural progressives in the Democratic party.

---

[8] *La Follette's Magazine,* VIII, No. 1 Jan. 1916.

[9] New York *Times,* April 6, 1915.

[10] White to Joseph Tumulty, Sept. 4, 1914, White Papers.

The first major effort of the pacifist forces in Congress, of which the insurgent Republicans were an important segment, was a campaign to establish an embargo on the export of munitions to the belligerent powers. In effect this meant the stopping of arms shipments to the Allies, since the British naval blockade effectively prevented arms reaching the Central Powers from America. The Wilson administration strenuously opposed such a move, and it was backed in its stand by Republican militants such as Lodge. In January 1915, pressure for the curbing of the arms trade reached such a point that Secretary of State Bryan felt it necessary to deny publicly that the United States was favoring the Allies by allowing the trade to continue. Under international law, Bryan pointed out, it was the duty of the belligerents to stop contraband. The United States was not obliged to do so, merely because one of the belligerent powers had greater naval strength.[11]

In Congress, Lodge defended the administration's stand on this point. Certainly the government had the power to place an embargo on the export of arms, Lodge admitted. But such a step would be an unneutral act, for it would involve a neutral power deliberately changing "a condition created by the war," thereby benefiting one belligerent at the expense of the other. "Here it so happens that the conditions of the war have given the control of the sea to what are usually called 'the allies.' Now if we undertake to undo that condition we of course at once to that extent make ourselves the ally of Germany." [12]

Critics of the arms trade on the other hand argued that allowing it to continue placed the United States on the side of the Allies. "How long," asked La Follette rhetorically, "can we maintain a semblance of real neutrality while we are supplying the Allies with munitions of war and the money to prosecute war?" [13] From the moment the American government acquiesced in the British blockade of Germany but allowed the flow of arms to the Allies to continue, Senator Works argued,

11 New York *Times,* Jan. 25, 1915.

12 *Cong. Record,* 64 Cong., 1 Session, Jan. 5, 1916, p. 509.

13 *La Follette's Magazine,* VII, No. 9, Sept. 1915.

"we . . . practically made ourselves parties to the war by supplying munitions of war and money to one side of the controversy, while neither is being furnished to the other side. We are not neutral." [14]

In fact both sides were right. America could not remain completely neutral in the war. Any action taken by the United States would benefit one side or the other. However the flow of arms to the Allies was a highly visible sign of American involvement, and it raised the vision of Europeans being killed by guns made in America. The insurgents accused the armaments manufacturers of involving the United States in the World War for the sake of the profits they made from the arms trade. "It is repugnant to every moral sense," La Follette declared in February 1915, "that Governments should even indirectly be drawn into making and prosecuting a war through the machinations of those who make money by it." [15]

On February 18, 1915, Senator Hitchcock, a Nebraska Democrat, moved an amendment to the Ship Purchase bill providing for an arms embargo. It was defeated 51 to 36, all the progressive Republicans present voting for it except Sterling. Even Borah and Poindexter supported the ban on this roll call.[16] The issue never came to a vote again, though the pacifist forces continued to push for it. When the Sixty-fourth Congress convened in December 1915, Senator Kenyon was denied a place on the Foreign Relations committee, reportedly because of his advocacy of an embargo.[17] On January 27, 1916, Kenyon introduced a petition of more than one million signatures calling for an end to the arms trade. Several Senators including Clapp and Works spoke in favor of the idea, and an attempt was made to have the petition referred to the Commerce committee where it was expected to receive more favorable treatment than in the Foreign Relations committee.[18] But the attempt failed, and the issue died for ever.

---

[14] *Cong. Record,* 64 Cong., 1 Session, Jan. 5, 1916, p. 507.

[15] *Ibid.,* 63 Cong., 3 Session, Feb. 12, 1915, p. 3633.

[16] *Ibid.,* 63 Cong., 3 Session, Feb. 18, 1915, p. 4016.

[17] New York *Times,* Dec. 12, 1915.

[18] *Ibid.,* Jan. 28, 1916.

A more difficult issue for the insurgents and the pacifist forces in general to handle was the explosive question of submarine warfare, which was eventually to lead the United States into war with Germany. Like most other Americans, the insurgents were horrified at the sinking of the British liner, the *Lusitania,* by a German submarine on May 7, 1915, with the loss of nearly 1200 lives. Cummins and Kenyon were among those who praised the President's note to Germany which protested this "indescribable violation of international rules." [19] Yet at the same time the insurgents were not entirely happy with the way the administration handled the submarine issue. The President's note was "excellent as a protest," Senator Works commented, "but the important question is, What is to come after?" [20] There could be no justification for a war with Germany on such an issue, "considering our own grave fault in supplying arms and munitions of war to the belligerents and especially in allowing passengers to travel on a belligerent ship carrying arms and munitions of war." [21]

One way out of the danger appeared to be for the United States government to warn or prohibit American citizens from travelling on ships that might be attacked by German submarines. The government, Senator Works charged, had been well aware that the *Lusitania,* on its fateful voyage, had been "loaded to the guards with arms and munitions of war for some of the belligerent nations." It was not just the passengers themselves who were at fault, therefore, "but the Government, in permitting passengers to take passage upon a ship that was practically carrying death and destruction to the subjects of one of the contending nations, is to some extent morally responsible for the deaths." As a "mere question of law," Works said, there was no question of the right of Americans to travel on such ships, but "certainly there is a moral responsibility resting not only upon the Government but upon every American citizen . . . to avoid conflict with the nations that are now at war." [22]

[19] *Ibid.,* May 15, 1915.
[20] *Ibid.*
[21] *Ibid.,* June 1, 1915.
[22] *Cong. Record,* 64 Cong., 1 Session, Jan. 5, 1916, p. 507.

In December 1915, Senator Kenyon introduced a resolution which would have forbidden the issue of clearance papers to ships carrying munitions of war if passengers were to be carried in the same ships,[23] but the issue really came to a head in February 1916 when the German government announced it was about to order its submarines to attack all armed belligerent merchantmen without warning. A few days later Secretary Lansing told reporters that the government would not warn its citizens against traveling on such ships or insist on the Allies disarming its vessels. As Arthur Link has written, this announcement set off an explosion in Congress. In the House, Representative McLemore, a Democrat from Texas, introduced a resolution warning Americans against travel on armed belligerent ships, and Senator Gore of Oklahoma introduced a similar resolution in the Senate.[24]

To meet this challenge, Wilson threw the whole force of his influence as President and party leader against the resolutions. The country's newspapers strongly supported the President's stand, and administrative patronage was used effectively to bring errant Democrats into line. Under this pressure the opposition wilted considerably, but the progressive Republicans stood solidly for the resolutions. In the House, 93 Republicans supported the President, but they were nearly all from the eastern, conservative wing of the party. The congressional delegations from Iowa, Wisconsin, Nebraska, and Minnesota, the heartland of Republican insurgency, voted against the administration to a man.[25] Seven of the fourteen Senators voting in favor of the Gore resolution were progressive Republicans.[26] When in April 1916 the President delivered a strongly-worded ultimatum to Germany threatening to break off diplomatic relations if the submarine policies continued, Senator Kenyon

[23] New York *Times,* Dec. 14, 1915.
[24] Link, *Wilson and the Progressive Era,* pp. 210–213.
[25] New York *Times,* March 8 and 9, 1916.
[26] They were Borah, Clapp, Cummins, Gronna, La Follette, Norris, and Works. This roll call must be interpreted cautiously since the parliamentary situation at the time was so confused that some Senators were not sure what they were voting for. Gore voted to table his own resolution. New York *Times,* March 4, 1916.

commented, "If war comes out of this, I hope that the first to enlist will be those who insisted on riding on armed belligerent ships." [27]

Closely linked to the controversies over the export of arms and submarine warfare was the question of American military "preparedness." Soon after the European war broke out, some Americans who favored U. S. intervention began to press for a program of increased armaments for the United States. The tempo of this campaign increased rapidly during the early months of 1915, and the country was bombarded with a flood of propaganda depicting the dangers of America's military weakness and the possibilities of foreign invasion. The progressive Republicans, along with other pacifistic groups, took a grim view of the preparedness agitation. The fact that its supporters included many leading representatives of big business interests seemed to confirm their view that a "war trust" was attempting to involve the United States in a military program and perhaps even in the European war itself, for the sake of financial gain.[28] "Back of every big army and navy appropriation bill," La Follette wrote in his magazine in February 1915, "is the organized power of private interest." [29] In November La Follette backed up this charge with a demonstration that the Navy League's list of sponsors read like a Who's Who of American corporate finance.[30] The antipreparedness progressives continually hammered on this aspect of the question.

When President Wilson turned preparedness into a live political issue by calling for an expansion of the armed forces in November 1915, the response of the progressive Republicans was not wholly negative. The trouble was, as Senator Norris put it, "There seems to be a preparedness germ or an epidemic that has swept the country. Nearly everyone has it." [31] Norris himself did not swerve from outright opposition to

[27] New York *Times,* April 20, 1916.
[28] Joseph Bristow to Thomas R. Marshall, Sept. 14, 1915, Bristow Papers.
[29] *La Follette's Magazine,* VII, No. 2, Feb. 1915.
[30] *Ibid.,* VII, No. 11, Nov. 1915.
[31] New York *Times,* Nov. 13, 1915.

preparedness, but more cautious politicians like Albert Cummins hesitated to commit themselves against a program which seemed to have such widespread support, especially with a presidential election around the corner. He was in favor of "such preparedness, both on land and sea, as is necessary," Senator Cummins declared.[32] No doubt Cummins was anxious at this stage to avoid placing himself at odds with the eastern Republicans on yet another major issue, in the midst of his attempt to win the presidential nomination.

As a result of such "political" factors, progressive Republican criticism of the administration's preparedness program was rather muted and selective, and it was the rural-pacifist wing of the Democratic party that gave Wilson the most trouble on this issue. In the Senate, Cummins took the lead in championing the cause of the National Guard over the proposed "continental army," but he was careful to emphasize that he was "heartily in favor of the [army] bill generally." [33] Senator Clapp praised the Committee on Military Affairs for introducing "such a moderate bill" considering "the pressure that has been put upon them." [34] Otherwise the insurgents took little part in the Senate debate on the army bill, only Works of California attacking the measure as totally unnecessary.[35]

However, the big navy bill that was introduced in the Senate drew heavy fire from the Republican insurgents, with Norris and Works leading the attack.[36] One Norris amendment provided that no work be begun on the construction of battleships until the President had made an effort to negotiate an international arbitration treaty.[37] Clapp, Cummins, Gronna, Kenyon, and La Follette supported this proposal, but only a handful of other Senators voted for it.[38]

Typically, Cummins attempted to find a middle position on

[32] *Ibid.*, Oct. 18, 1915.
[33] *Cong. Record,* 64 Cong., 1 Session, April 3, 1916, p. 5353.
[34] *Ibid.*, p. 5368.
[35] *Ibid.*, April 12, 1916, pp. 5938–5940.
[36] New York *Times,* July 18, 1916.
[37] *Cong. Record,* 64 Cong., 1 Session, July 17, 1916, p. 11185.
[38] *Ibid.*, p. 11192.

the navy bill. He favored moderate increases in the size of the army and navy, he said, but he did not want a belligerent foreign policy, and he attacked those whose interest in preparedness sprang from a profit motive. "I believe that we ought to build first class battleships, some of them; we ought to build first class battle cruisers, some of them," Cummins said cautiously.[39] The navy bill under consideration, he warned, "will destroy in large measure, our influence for peace when the opportunity comes to exert that influence," but nevertheless he was "unwilling to cast a vote against the reasonable preparedness of the Nation." [40] Cummins made an attempt to prune the naval bill to "reasonable" proportions by an amendment which would have cut the number of new battleships from ten to two, and battle cruisers from six to four. Only fourteen Senators supported this amendment, seven of whom were progressive Republicans.[41] On the final roll call Cummins and Kenyon chose to support the bill on the grounds that too much preparedness was better than too little, but five insurgents voted against it along with two Democrats and one conservative Republican from Kansas.[42]

The inclination of the insurgents to favor pacifistic, non-interventionist foreign policies in 1915 and 1916 was not, in itself, a political handicap. A large section of the Democratic party took a similar position on the international issues of the day, and many conservative Republicans from western states criticized Wilson for being overbelligerent in foreign affairs. Moreover, it is generally agreed by historians that a major factor in Wilson's presidential victory of 1916 was the success of the party's slogan, "He kept us out of the War."

Nevertheless the rise of these international issues in 1915 and 1916 undoubtedly weakened the Republican insurgents as a force in national politics, for they now found themselves chained to a party that was not only dominated by conserva-

---

[39] *Ibid.,* July 19, 1916, p. 11312.
[40] *Ibid.,* p. 11313.
[41] *Ibid.,* July 21, 1916, pp. 11366–11367.
[42] *Ibid.,* p. 11384.

tism on domestic affairs, but one whose leading spokesmen on foreign policy were militant interventionists. Once again the two wings of the Republican party were attacking the Democratic administration from diametrically opposed positions.

The intrusion of foreign policy issues into American politics underlined the insurgents' political dilemma. There was nothing inherently weakening about advocating a pacifistic foreign policy in 1915 and 1916, but it was a severe political problem for those who were committed to a national party led, on foreign affairs, by Henry Cabot Lodge and Elihu Root.

# chapter ten

# The Independents:
# Norris and La Follette

It is impossible to make generalizations about the political behavior of the progressive Republicans in the Taft and Wilson years without making constant references to the aberrant behavior of this or that insurgent on one issue or another. In some cases it becomes questionable whether a particular Congressman or Senator can be reasonably classed as a progressive at all. Thomas Sterling of South Dakota, for example, referred to himself as a progressive during his campaign for a Senate seat in 1912 and endorsed Theodore Roosevelt for President even after Roosevelt had bolted the Republican party.[1] Once in the Senate, Sterling's speeches revealed that deep suspicion of corporate power that so characterized the thinking of rural progressives at the time. Yet Sterling denounced big government almost as often as he attacked big business in the Wilson years, and his views on foreign policy resembled those of Lodge rather than La Follette. It is impossible to categorize such a man simply as a "progressive" or a "conservative."

Peripheral figures like Sterling aside, there was considerable variation of political behavior and belief among the insurgent Republicans. Diversity of this kind would not normally call for any special comment, for to boast a record of political in-

---

[1] Sterling to Coe Crawford, July 31, 1912, Crawford Papers.

dependence has always been one of the most commonplace stratagems in American politics. The Republican insurgents, imbued as they were with strong feelings about the value of political individualism and the evils of machine control, were perhaps less inclined than most to accept external discipline or to act willingly in concert as a group. Nevertheless two of the most outstanding insurgent Republicans, George W. Norris of Nebraska and Robert M. La Follette of Wisconsin, must be discussed separately in this context, for these two men came to adopt postures of political independence not just as an occasional tactic, but as a total strategy.

Before the Wilson years, the political style of George Norris did not differ remarkably from that of other leading Republican insurgents; indeed, Norris's early career fits the progressive Republican stereotype rather closely. Like La Follette, Cummins, Crawford, Bristow, Dolliver, and many others, Norris was a small-town lawyer from a rural Republican state who entered politics in the 1880's as a regular Republican. Though Populism and Bryanism swept his state and his local district in the 1890's, Norris's loyalty to conservative Republicanism did not falter in this decade. In 1902 Norris won the Republican nomination for a Congressional seat, partly on the strength of his earlier victories over Populists and Bryanite Democrats.[2]

At no point in his political career did Norris attempt to build a personal political machine of his own,[3] but neither were his first years in Congress marked by any strong tendency towards independence. He entered Congress, Norris wrote in his autobiography, as "a bitter Republican partisan," [4] and it was not until his third term in the House that he sided with the insurgents who were attacking the power of Speaker Cannon. Indeed, at the end of his first term in office, Norris praised Cannon's leadership and declared that his "able, honest, and wise administration," had been "one of the great elements" in

---

[2] Lowitt, *Norris,* Chapters 4, 7, 8, and 9.

[3] *Ibid.,* p. 130.

[4] George W. Norris, *Fighting Liberal: the Autobiography of George W. Norris* (New York, 1945), p. 103.

the Republican victory of 1904.[5] In that year Cannon spoke
on Norris's behalf in the election campaign, and two years
later Norris hoped that he would do so again.[6] No single act
marked the emergence of Norris as a full-fledged insurgent.
Rather his swing toward progressive policies and independence of the Republican organization in the House paralleled
President Roosevelt's movement to the left and the general
drift of public opinion in Nebraska and the neighboring states.

To this point, Norris's political career had been quite typical of a progressive Republican leader in this period, and he
did not deviate remarkably from the general pattern of insurgent activity during the years of the Taft administration.
Norris's attacks on the Cannon machine and his disinclination
to form a permanent alliance with the Democrats in 1910
reflected the general progressive Republican attitude at the
time. In 1911 Norris became a leading supporter of Senator
La Follette for the presidency and later, like nearly all the
insurgents, switched his support to Theodore Roosevelt. After
the Republican convention of 1912, Norris refused to join the
third party but endorsed Roosevelt's presidential candidacy on
the third party ticket. In its broad outlines, Norris's political
career up to 1912 exemplifies the course of the whole insurgent
movement up to that date.

But even then Norris had begun to lay particular stress in
both word and action on one particular aspect of the progressive Republican rhetoric — the value of political individualism
and the evils of partisanship. As a group whose primary political problem was its inability to find a satisfactory place in
the existing party system, the insurgents were naturally inclined to disparage political parties in general and machine
control of parties in particular. Up to 1912 insurgent rhetoric
along these lines was directed mainly against "Cannonism"
and "Aldrichism" within the Republican party, whereas after
1913 it was generally Democrats who came under fire as "slaves
of the caucus" and Wilson's sycophants. Certainly Norris was

[5] Quoted in Lowitt, *Norris,* p. 93.
[6] *Ibid.,* pp. 92, 110.

not alone in his constant attacks on the power of political machines and the irrational partisanship of voters.

Yet the great majority of progressive Republicans were far too partisan themselves to give up the notion of party altogether. While they might occasionally resign themselves to "an independent attitude," as Bristow did in the bleak days that followed the election of 1912, they continued to seek ways of working within the party system and to assert that the Republican party provided the most effective medium for the advancement of the progressive cause. Thus La Follette, in his autobiography of 1912, while castigating the standpat politicians who dominated the Republican party nationally, asserted that the party itself was progressive and that progressives should stay inside the organization while fighting for their own kind of policies.[7] Cummins, attempting to find common ground with the conservatives during his bid for the presidential nomination in 1916, stressed issues like the tariff on which Republicans of all factions could agree and went so far as to speak of "the coherence of Republican thought." [8]

Norris, on the other hand, moved steadily toward a total rejection of parties *per se* in the Wilson years, a process that eventually culminated in his decision of 1936 to drop all pretense of party affiliation and run for re-election to the Senate as an avowed Independent. In the period under consideration, Norris had not gone nearly so far in the direction of open independence, but already he was urging voters to scratch party tickets and choose the best men for office irrespective of party. The country needed "a sentiment that shall applaud rather than condemn any citizen who shall oppose his party whenever in his own heart he believes such action best for good government," Norris declared in December 1913.[9] "I have almost learned to be suspicious of anything that is connected with any political party," he had confided the year

---

[7] La Follette, *Autobiography*, p. 320.

[8] Manuscript for speech, some time in 1915, Cummins Papers.

[9] Quoted in Alfred Lief, *Democracy's Norris, The Biography of a Lonely Crusade* (New York, 1939), p. 146.

previously,[10] and it became clear in the Wilson years that he was taking this strand of the progressive ideology much more seriously than his fellow insurgents.

La Follette's concept of a political party as something other than the organization that controlled it was of no comfort to Norris, and he rejected as unrealistic the notion of parties as groups of men committed to the advocacy of shared beliefs and principles. Instead Norris talked of political parties as though they were indistinguishable from machine organizations, which in turn were invariably linked to private interests with malignant purposes. He did not articulate these beliefs as part of any overall political theory. They were just assumptions he made whenever the role of partisanship in national affairs was under discussion. Writing of the after-effects of the Cannon fight in his autobiography, for instance, Norris observed, "It left appointment of the standing committees largely to the partisan machines. It left the deliberations largely to powerful monopolies." [11] The organization of the House along party lines automatically implied the dominance of monopoly! This judgement was written much later, in the 1940's, but Norris seems to have already adopted such views in the Wilson years.

One might have supposed that Wilson's adroit use of the Democratic party machine and Congressional caucus for the enactment of his program of reform would have convinced Norris that party organization and progressivism were not necessarily antithetical forces. Instead Wilson's legislative methods turned Norris against the President's program and against Wilson personally, for he held the President to be chiefly responsible for the actions of the Democratic majorities in Congress. "A public official should in the performance of his official duties be entirely non-partisan," Norris wrote years later. Whenever he casts a vote "that is not in harmony with his own conscientious conviction, then the party spirit has become the instrument of injury to the body politic rather

---

10 Norris to N. N. Ayers, March 29, 1912, Norris Papers.
11 Norris, *Fighting Liberal*, p. 131.

than a blessing. . . . it is in this way that bad laws are placed on the statute books." [12] Independent voting led to good laws and party voting to bad laws; it was as simple as that.

In the Wilson years, Norris had not yet made an open break with the Republican party, as he was to do later. Moreover, he had no more sympathy for Wilson and the Democratic majority than his fellow insurgents, and like them he voted against most of the administration's major bills. Nevertheless the emphasis that Norris had begun to place on political individualism was not solely a matter of rhetoric, as was made clear by his attitude toward the Progressive party in the crucial elections of 1914. To strategists like Borah and Cummins, it seemed vitally important that the third party should not survive this test and that the bolters of 1912 should be brought back within the Republican fold in time to strengthen the progressive wing of the party before the national convention of 1916. Bull Moosers like Albert Beveridge and William Allen White also saw these elections as a test between the Progressives and the progressive Republicans, and they did their best to see that Cummins and others of his ilk were defeated. In the midst of this struggle, believed on both sides to be a fight to the death, Norris calmly announced that he would campaign for prominent Bull Moose candidates in certain crucial states. In Illinois Norris endorsed Raymond Robins, the Progressive party nominee for Senator, who was running against a self-styled progressive Republican, Lawrence Y. Sherman.[13] In Pennsylvania Norris campaigned for the Bull Mooser, Gifford Pinchot, who was opposing the reactionary Republican Senator, Boies Penrose.[14] These actions must have horrified Cummins and Borah, who were preaching the lesson that the Republican party offered the only satisfactory vehicle for progressive reform. But to Norris the issue was quite simple; good

---

[12] George W. Norris, "Why I Believe in the Direct Primary," *Annals of the American Academy of Political and Social Science*, CVI, No. 193, March 1923, p. 23.
[13] New York *Times*, Oct. 6, 1914; *La Follette's Weekly*, V, No. 15, April 12, 1913.
[14] New York *Times*, Oct. 20, 1914.

men must be supported irrespective of party considerations. His only regret about the Pennsylvania situation, he said, was that all those who opposed Penrose, including the Democrats, could not have agreed to support a single candidate.[15]

There is certainly something magnificent about the political independence of George Norris. One cannot but admire his insistence on supporting whatever men and measures he believed in, irrespective of the political consequences; nor can one quarrel with Richard L. Neuberger and S. B. Kahn for entitling their biography *Integrity, the Life of George Norris.* Yet Norris's rejection of parties as modes of political expression was scarcely an adequate answer to the problems of the insurgent Republicans or for that matter, of any other political group. In the realm of theory alone, the naivety of his notions of party are obvious enough. To depict American politics as a battle between the pressures of "party" on the one hand and "conscience" on the other is clearly a gross distortion of reality. Why must party always be the handmaiden of "the interests" and the enemy of the official's conscience, as Norris invariably assumed? If party loyalties exerted no pressure on a legislator, would "conscience" be left in sole command of the field? Would the average politician be more or less subject to nefarious influences without party organization and party principles to sustain him? Above all, how are issues to be presented to the public in a meaningful way except through the medium of party platforms and party leaders?

Though Norris's own career is an example of political individualism at its finest, his resort to this style of political behavior must be seen, in the last analysis, as a product of the frustration of the progressive movement within the Republican party. In his conservative days Norris had not been particularly concerned with the evils of partisanship. Clearly his strong views on the subject developed as a corollary of his growing commitment to progressivism during the Roosevelt and Taft administrations. Basically Norris came to dislike parties because the existing party structure balked his efforts to

---

[15] *Ibid.*

advance the progressive cause. He condemned progressive Democrats for not sharing his views on party in the years of Taft and Wilson.[16] But the progressive Democrats had little reason to reject their party at this time. Under the leadership of Bryan and Wilson they had taken control of their party at the very moment when the Old Guard was successfully fending off the insurgent assaults in the Republican party. Certainly the Democrats were inclined to be "slaves of the caucus" in these years, but under Wilson the Democratic party's Congressional caucus had come to be the most effective instrument of progressive reform in national politics. Unable to repeat this performance, the progressive Republicans were reduced to a series of devious and ultimately futile maneuvers in the Wilson years. By rejecting the idea of working through a party at all, Norris was confessing that the attempt to make the Republican party progressive had been a failure.

Like Norris, Robert La Follette became in the latter part of his career one of the great independents in American politics, but beyond that, the political styles of the two men had little in common. The basis of La Follette's individualism seems to have been his inability to work in harmony with any group of politicians who did not accept him as their unquestioned leader. "He was entirely unable to do teamwork," one of his early supporters in state politics, Nils P. Haugen, wrote later. "He must have his way or stop the machine." Haugen noted that La Follette broke with nearly all his important associates from the Wisconsin days "for no apparent reason except that La Follette desired more subserviency in his supporters." [17] A letter of Joseph Bristow's, written in 1909 when he was a freshman senator, provides insight and a more disinterested picture of La Follette's personality and the way it affected his political style. La Follette, Bristow noted,

> is a crusader, the ablest of all the progressive Senators; a tireless worker, bold and fearless and reckless as a fighter, giving nor ask-

16 Lowitt, *Norris*, p. 224.
17 Nils P. Haugen, "Pioneer and Political Reminiscences," *Wisconsin Magazine of History*, XII, No. 3, March 1929, p. 280.

ing favor or quarter; but a very sensitive and retiring individual from the social point of view. He doesn't mingle with the other Senators much; is exceedingly cordial to those he likes, vindictive and defiant to those whom he doesn't like. He spends every leisure moment in his rooms at work, while the majority of the other Senators visit together in the cloakrooms and lunch room, and talk over different phases of national questions. While they are doing this, La Follette is down in his committee rooms digging out the details of some questions of legislation. The result is that he never will be influential personally in the Senate, though he will always be the master in the discussion of questions, because he will know more about them than anybody else.[18]

The sensitivity and vindictiveness toward political opponents that Bristow commented on in 1909 did not as yet create an insurmountable barrier between La Follette and the other insurgents, although some of them already resented his attempts to dominate the movement.[19] As the first and most famous of the progressive Republican Governors and as the outstanding insurgent in the Senate, La Follette commanded the respect and admiration of most progressive Republicans. With the death of Dolliver and the defeat of Beveridge in 1910, the insurgents were in general agreement that La Follette was the obvious man to lead the fight against Taft's renomination in 1912.[20]

But serious troubles arose in the early months of 1912 when it became clear that La Follette's presidential boom was failing and that progressive Republicans were looking toward Theodore Roosevelt to take over the fight against Taft. The stronger supporters of La Follette, men like Norris and Bristow, did not expect him to drop out of the race as soon as the Roosevelt boom got under way. But they did expect that La Follette would try to avoid clashes between his supporters and the Roosevelt forces — a development that might open the door to a dangerous split in the progressive forces and an

---

[18] Bristow to C. B. Kirkland, March 20, 1909, Bristow Papers.
[19] Coe Crawford to Theodore Roosevelt, August 15, 1910, Roosevelt Papers.
[20] See p. 49 above.

easy Taft victory. Far from cooperating with Roosevelt's supporters, however, La Follette began a series of slashing public
attacks on the Colonel, denouncing him as a traitor to the
progressive cause and condemning him for breaking an alleged
commitment to support La Follette's candidacy.

These charges were spelled out most fully in La Follette's
*Autobiography*, which first appeared in serial form in the
*American Magazine* during 1911 and 1912. La Follette claimed
that Roosevelt had encouraged him to get in the presidential
race in 1911 in order to test Taft's strength, intending all
along "to displace the candidate put out against Taft" if it
became clear that the President could be beaten in the convention.[21] He also asserted that Roosevelt was not and never
had been truly committed to the progressive cause, citing as
evidence Roosevelt's attitude to the trusts, his opposition to
the Wisconsin progressives during their early struggles against
the conservative state machine, and the numerous instances in
which Roosevelt as President had compromised or side-stepped
progressive issues such as railroad regulation and tariff revision.[22]

La Follette described the issue as a case of principle versus
expediency. Progressive Republicans were switching their support to Roosevelt simply because they thought Roosevelt a
more likely winner, La Follette charged, and such a course
of action was bound to have disastrous results. To compromise on a candidate or a principle "not only weakens the cause
for which you are contending but destroys confidence in your
constancy of purpose." [23] And the principled course of action
in this case, as in every other, was to support La Follette to
the bitter end. "I had gone into the campaign as a candidate,"
he wrote in 1912, "believing that I had been so identified with
the Progressive movement that my candidacy was one with it."
To desert La Follette was to desert progressivism.[24]

If victory was not to be had without compromise and with-

---

[21] La Follette, *Autobiography*, Chapter 11, especially pp. 218–219.
[22] *Ibid.*, Chapter 11.
[23] *Ibid.*, p. 223.
[24] *Ibid.*, p. 285.

out La Follette as the unchallenged leader, La Follette preferred outright defeat. Indeed he seemed to derive a certain masochistic pleasure from his isolation and his defeats. "Alone in the Senate" is the title La Follette gave to the chapter of his autobiography dealing with his first years in national politics. And writing of the attack on the Payne-Aldrich tariff bill, he says, "The consideration of the tariff bill had proceeded but a little way when it became certain that no important changes would be affected. But that did not deter the Progressives. Defeated again and again, they returned to the attack. It was a splendid exhibition of the true spirit of moral reform. *Defeat was a matter of no consequence to them.*" [25] The other insurgents would not have denied that there were occasions on which it was better to lose a fight by sticking to principle than to win a meaningless victory through compromise, but La Follette went further than any of them in this direction. Norris, for instance, though he was unwilling to compromise his integrity by supporting men and measures he disapproved of, was quite willing to accept the kind of "half loaf" legislative compromises which La Follette condemned so violently. On the Federal Trade Commission bill, for example, Norris declared that although he did not approve of the measure entirely and thought he could have devised a superior plan, he was "willing to take anything that offers a fair chance of being successful." [26] La Follette preferred to go down fighting for an unsullied and unattainable bill.

On the crucial question of his presidential candidacy, La Follette got almost no support for the position he adopted in 1912. "I have always been for La Follette in preference to Roosevelt," Bristow wrote in March 1912, "but I don't like the way he is acting. He seems to be fighting Roosevelt as much as Taft, and while I think La Follette is a better progressive than Roosevelt, yet Roosevelt is so much better than Taft that every friend of La Follette's ought to support Roosevelt where Roosevelt is the stronger." [27] If the question were put to him,

---

[25] *Ibid.,* p. 191. La Follette's italics.
[26] *Cong. Record,* 63 Cong., 2 Session, July 3, 1914, p. 11597.
[27] Bristow to R. A. Harris, March 20, 1912, Bristow Papers.

George Norris said, he would feel compelled to criticize La Follette for the course he had taken.[28] If La Follette had announced his support for Roosevelt, Norris believed, he would have been invincible four years later.[29] William Allen White warned that it would be a serious mistake for La Follette to join Taft in attacking Roosevelt.[30] All these men — Norris, Bristow, and White — had been strong supporters of La Follette in 1911 and had not switched their support to Roosevelt until it had become abundantly clear that La Follette had no chance of winning the nomination.

If the progressive Republicans were disturbed by La Follette's attacks on Roosevelt in the early months of 1912, they were outraged and angered by his actions at the convention itself. In an effort to unite the progressive forces, Roosevelt had chosen as his candidate for temporary chairman of the convention Governor Francis E. McGovern of Wisconsin.[31] But when McGovern's name was placed in nomination, La Follette's manager Walter Houser stood up and repudiated McGovern's candidacy on behalf of La Follette.[32] Nor would La Follette consent to the release of his 41 delegates to Roosevelt, which some progressives such as Henry Allen of Kansas believed would have turned the tide against Taft.[33]

The breach established between La Follette and the rest of the progressive Republican movement in 1912 was not healed for many years. La Follette had not only attacked Roosevelt in the most bitter terms; but he had also condemned all those who supported him, singling out some of the men who had once held him in the highest regard, for special attention.[34] He was particularly hostile to Albert Cummins for announcing

---

[28] Norris to J. J. McCarthy, March 25, 1912, Norris Papers.
[29] Norris to M. E. Wells, Feb. 29, 1912, *ibid.*
[30] White to Charles R. Van Hise, May 24, 1912, White Papers.
[31] Mowry, *Theodore Roosevelt and the Progressive Movement,* p. 242.
[32] Robert S. Maxwell, *La Follette and the Rise of the Progressives in Wisconsin* (Madison, Wis., 1956), pp. 187–188; La Follette, *La Follette,* p. 439.
[33] J. R. Harrison to Joseph Bristow, July 16, 1912, Bristow Papers.
[34] See, for example, La Follette's reference to William Allen White, *Autobiography,* p. 247.

his own presidential candidacy after he had earlier promised to support La Follette.[35]

In national affairs, La Follette was no longer the influential figure after 1912 that he had been during the years of Taft's administration, since he had cut himself off to a considerable extent from the mainstream of the progressive Republican movement, which he had once led. What influence he did retain he did not use to its maximum advantage. In the election campaign of 1912, for example, La Follette endorsed none of the three major candidates.[36] *La Follette's Magazine* did carry an article by Senator Works urging progressives to vote for Wilson, but La Follette made no major effort on behalf of the Democratic candidate.

Insofar as he did offer any strategy for progressive Republicans after 1912, La Follette's advice was to continue the fight within the Republican party, but this was intended mainly as a slap at Roosevelt's third party. La Follette took no important part in the efforts of Cummins, Borah, and others to strengthen the position of the progressives in the G.O.P. Despite the attacks La Follette had made upon him, Cummins was anxious to involve the Wisconsin Senator in his "reorganization" plan of 1913;[37] but La Follette would have no part of a movement led by Cummins, and he refused to attend the conference of insurgents held at Chicago in June 1913.[38] What is more, La Follette's continual attacks on Roosevelt and the third party tended to undercut the Cummins strategy, for though Cummins had hoped that the Bull Moose party would collapse, he did not wish to embitter relationships between Progressives and progressive Republicans to the point where future cooperation between them would be impossible. Even Borah, one of the most virulent critics of the Bull Moose party, refrained from attacks on Roosevelt himself and concentrated his fire on the more vulnerable figure of George Perkins.

Ideologically no great gulf separated La Follette from the

---

[35] *Ibid.*, pp. 221–226, 250–251.
[36] La Follette, *La Follette*, p. 450.
[37] New York *Times*, May 11, 1913.
[38] New York *Tribune*, May 6, 1913.

other insurgents, and on most of the major issues of the Wilson administration he voted and debated alongside them. Occasionally he even joined them in the close legislative strategy that had been the hallmark of the insurgent attacks on Aldrich and Cannon in the early days of the Taft administration. For instance, the insurgent Republican Senators including La Follette met to coordinate their stand on the Underwood tariff bill in 1913.[39] It was typical of La Follette, however, that he wound up voting with the Democrats on this issue while every other insurgent Senator opposed it. During the course of the debates La Follette had taken the occasion to denounce an amendment offered by Cummins incorporating the so-called "Iowa idea" that had first brought Cummins to national attention. This was a scheme for combating the trusts by denying them tariff protection. La Follette objected to it on the grounds that innocent workers would suffer for the misdeeds of their employers.[40]

This pattern lasted throughout Wilson's first presidential term. La Follette kept his distance from the other insurgents, voting with the Democrats more often than any of the others. Occasionally he broke openly with them, as when he attacked Cummins for voting against the confirmation of Brandeis to the Supreme Court in 1916.[41] Yet differences on issues were not so great as to have precluded a closer relationship. La Follette agreed with the other insurgents that the Democratic tariff discriminated against the western farmer, that the banking and anti-trust legislation was ineffective if not reactionary, and that involvement in the European war must be avoided at all costs.

Clearly it was not ideology that kept La Follette so isolated from his former associates and followers in the Wilson years. It was rather that he could not bring himself to work in close cooperation with the men who had deserted him in 1912. In particular he would not play a role subordinate to Albert B. Cummins. In 1915 and 1916 Cummins's presidential campaign

---

[39] La Follette, *La Follette*, p. 476.

[40] *Cong. Record*, 63 Cong., 1 Session, Sept. 9, 1913, p. 4567.

[41] *La Follette's Magazine*, VIII, No. 4, April 1916.

represented just the kind of movement that La Follette had always advocated — a fight for progressive principles within the Republican party — but La Follette did nothing to help the Cummins campaign. Instead he announced his own candidacy even though he did not expect to carry any states other than Wisconsin and North Dakota.[42]

In 1913 there was considerable speculation that La Follette was in the process of joining the Democrats. Though he had avoided open commitment to any candidate in the election, he seemed to lean toward Wilson more than any other candidate, and he was free with praise for William Jennings Bryan and other Democratic progressives.[43] Soon after Wilson's inauguration, La Follette had an interview with the President at the White House, and the press predicted that La Follette would become a close adviser of the administration.[44] Many observers saw La Follette's vote for the Underwood tariff later in the year as a first step toward open alignment with the Democratic party.[45] The general impression in the Senate was that he intended to go the whole way, Bristow reported in December 1913. "He confers with them [the Democrats] all of the time, much more so than he does with the progressive Republicans or Progressives," Bristow noted.[46]

La Follette was certainly much friendlier to the Wilson administration than any other prominent progressive Republican. Besides voting with the Democrats on such generally partisan measures as the tariff and the Adamson Railroad bill of 1916,[47] La Follette showed no hesitation in praising Wilson when he felt such praise was due. In February 1916, for example, La Follette wrote editorially that the appointment of Brandeis to the Supreme Court "must strengthen the confidence of all who love democracy in President Wilson." [48] Few

---

[42] La Follette, *La Follette,* p. 562.
[43] La Follette, *Autobiography,* p. 318.
[44] New York *Times,* March 14, 1913.
[45] *Ibid.,* Sept. 10, 1913.
[46] Bristow to Henry J. Allen, Dec. 6, 1913, Bristow Papers.
[47] *Cong. Record,* 64 Cong., 1 Session, Sept. 2, 1916, p. 13655.
[48] *La Follette's Magazine,* VIII, No. 2, Feb. 1916.

other Republicans would have made such a statement in an election year.

However, La Follette's willingness to support the Wilson administration on occasions did not signify an intention to move into the Democratic party but was rather a sign that he did not intend to be bound by any party ties. La Follette could not accept Wilson's leadership any more than he could Roosevelt's or Cummins's. He agreed with the main insurgent criticisms of Wilson and was particularly resentful of the fact that Democrats who "haven't been long enough interested in progressive principles . . . to be ready for the work" were drawing up legislation "independently of Progressives who have spent years on these subjects." [49] Though La Follette bore Wilson no personal ill will, he felt him to be "cocksure and stubborn while his inexperience and ignorance of more than the merest smattering on the problems, and his intense political partisan feeling renders him almost impossible." [50] Publicly La Follette took the stand that the progressive Republicans should not "play politics" with the Wilson administration but should support it when it was right and oppose it when it was wrong.[51] Privately he congratulated himself that he had maintained his independence.[52]

Thus, despite some early indications to the contrary, La Follette did not make an alliance with the Democrats in the Wilson years; and because he had also rejected the Progressive party and withdrawn from close relations with the Republican insurgents, he emerged as an isolated, independent figure in American politics. The theoretical basis for this independence was La Follette's view that it was better in the long run to make an outright fight for progressive principles than to make compromises for the sake of immediate results. Yet while this position was tenable, it could scarcely justify such actions as La Follette's refusal to endorse either presidential candidate in 1916. Immediately after the Republican convention, La Fol-

---

[49] Quoted in La Follette, *La Follette,* p. 488.
[50] Quoted, *ibid.,* p. 500.
[51] *La Follette's Weekly,* V, No. 14, April 5, 1913.
[52] La Follette, *La Follette,* p. 462.

lette did have some warm things to say about the Republican candidate, Charles Evans Hughes,[53] but in the course of the campaign La Follette clearly changed his mind as Hughes surrounded himself with conservative advisers and accused Wilson of not being militant enough in his foreign policy. After the election La Follette wrote in his magazine that Wilson's victory signified that "the plain people throughout the country registered their approval of his worthy efforts to keep this nation out of the maelstrom of war" and that western progressives would not vote for a candidate backed by the reactionary Old Guard.[54] If this was the significance of the election, why did not La Follette openly endorse Wilson as the more desirable candidate? Such an endorsement might have enabled Wilson to carry Wisconsin in an election where the margin of victory was extremely narrow. La Follette would have compromised nothing by such a statement, and his silence can only be explained on the basis of political expediency or his reluctance to commit himself to any cause save one led by himself.

La Follette's early supporters could never wholly admire him for his independence, for they believed it to be based on his egocentricity. Bristow thought that La Follette would never support any candidate for the Republican presidential nomination in 1916 other than himself.[55] William Allen White referred to La Follette's "temperamental limitations." [56] Senator Kenyon, in a letter to Borah in 1915, regretted that La Follette "has put himself in rather an unfortunate position," while in the next sentence he referred to Norris as "one of the best creations that the Lord ever put up." [57] Praise for Norris, pity for La Follette.

There was a negative quality to La Follette's independence

---

[53] *La Follette's Magazine*, VIII, No. 6, June 1915.

[54] *Ibid.*, VIII, No. 11, Nov. 1916.

[55] Bristow to Henry J. Allen, Dec. 6, 1913, Bristow Papers.

[56] William Allen White to Charles McCarthy, May 27, 1915, White Papers.

[57] William S. Kenyon to William E. Borah, May 25, 1915, Borah Papers.

that was altogether different from the Norris brand of individualism. Typically, while Norris broke party ranks to support Bull Moose candidates in 1914 and Democrats later on, La Follette demonstrated his independence by refusing to support any presidential candidate in 1912 and 1916 and by running for President himself on a third-party ticket in 1924. Norris moved gradually toward political independence as the progressive Republican movement gradually fell apart. But La Follette broke with his fellow progressives when the movement was at the peak of its power and influence. Arthur Link has spoken of the fragmentation of the progressive movement in the 1920's as a primary cause of its failure in the years of normalcy. La Follette must surely rank as one of the greatest fragmenters of the epoch.

# chapter eleven

# The Election of 1916

Woodrow Wilson won the presidential election of 1916, Arthur Link has argued convincingly, by identifying his candidacy with peace and progressivism.[1] No two causes meant more to the Republican insurgents than these; yet the election found most of the insurgents campaigning for Wilson's opponent, Charles Evans Hughes, in the company of America's most conservative and militaristic politicians. Thus the election of 1916 marks the ultimate failure of the Republican insurgents to find a satisfactory place in the party system. Of course the insurgents claimed that Hughes was more progressive than Wilson, but the contention cannot be taken seriously. Before the nominating convention they were not enthusiastic about Hughes, and an overwhelming majority of independent progressives supported Wilson. It was the bonds of partisanship, not ideological affinity, that kept the insurgents in the Hughes camp.

Could the insurgents have reasonably expected the nomination of a more acceptable candidate than Hughes, who after all was the most liberal Republican nominee for the presidency between the era of Theodore Roosevelt and the New Deal? No one could doubt that the events of 1912 had left the Old Guard in firm control of the Republican party, and the midterm elections of 1914 had strengthened the position of the

---

[1] Arthur S. Link, *Wilson: Campaigns for Progressivism and Peace, 1916–1917* (Princeton, 1965), Chapters 1–4, especially 108.

standpatters in the party. In that year the Republicans had made considerable gains in state and Congressional elections at the expense of the Democratic and Progressive parties. Most of these gains had been registered in eastern conservative states like New York, Pennsylvania, and New Jersey,[2] with traditional Republican issues like the tariff figuring prominently.[3] After this election, the national chairman of the Republican party had predicted that the Republicans would win the presidency in 1916 on the issues of the tariff and "Democratic legislation." [4] A Democratic Senator suggested that the logical Republican ticket for 1916 would be Boies Penrose of Pennsylvania and Cannon of Illinois.[5] The comment was intended merely as a political jibe, but it was not without point. The triumph of reactionary Republicans like Penrose and Cannon was one of the outstanding features of the 1914 elections. The G.O.P. appeared to be recovering from the debacle of 1912 without making any substantial concession to progressive doctrines.

Nevertheless, the insurgents were not without hope. Though the midterm elections had increased the strength of the conservative Republicans in Congress and the state houses while the progressive Republican position had remained static, another development seemed to have improved the strategic situation of the insurgents in national affairs. This was the virtual demise of the Progressive party in the midterm elections. The collapse of the third party everywhere except California not only seemed to justify the insurgents' decision to remain Republicans after 1912 but raised the vital question of whether one of the major parties could pick up the support of the Roosevelt voters of 1912. The outcome of the next presidential election seemed to depend on this issue, and the progressive Republicans believed they could capitalize on it to gain a position in the party disproportionate to their numerical strength. "There is no doubt that the Progressive party is

2 New York *Times,* Nov. 4, 1914.

3 *Ibid.,* Nov. 1, 1914.

4 *Ibid.,* Dec. 21, 1914.

5 *Ibid.,* Nov. 8, 1914.

slowly disintegrating as a party," Albert Cummins commented in April 1915, "but the question of where the Progressive influence will go depends upon the man the Republicans name for the Presidency. It may . . . go to the Democratic party if the man nominated by the Republicans does not fit the ideals of the Progressive movement." [6] The emphasis of this statement and others like it was intended to be on the final proviso. Borah's speeches in this period hammered on the same point. Wilson was a strong candidate, he warned in October 1915, but the Republican party could defeat him the following year if it "does a wise thing at Chicago and adopts a liberal platform." [7] Via such warnings as these the insurgents hoped to persuade the Old Guard to make concessions to the progressive wing of the party, even to the point of nominating an insurgent for the presidency.

Two insurgents were considered presidential possibilities in 1915 — Senators William E. Borah of Idaho and Albert B. Cummins of Iowa. Borah had many of the attributes necessary for a presidential candidate. His Senatorial career had earned him a national reputation, and he was reckoned to be one of the great political orators of his day. Though regarded as a progressive, Borah was more acceptable to the Old Guard of the party than men like Norris and Bristow. He had always been thoroughly regular on the tariff issue, even voting for the Payne-Aldrich bill of 1909, and his views on foreign policy were closer to those of Lodge and Root than to the pacifist midwestern point of view. Furthermore no one had attacked the Wilson administration and the Progressive party more vehemently than Borah.

Through 1915, Borah's name was often brought up as a minor possibility for the Republican presidential nomination. Many progressive Republicans and Bull Moosers urged him to make himself available as a candidate behind whom third party men and insurgent Republicans could unite. Henry Allen reported after an interview with Roosevelt in August 1915 that the Colonel would like to support Borah for the presidency in

[6] *Ibid.*, April 6, 1915.
[7] *Ibid.*, Oct. 10, 1915.

1916,[8] and though it is hard to believe that Roosevelt seriously intended to do any such thing, Allen's remark shows the drift of opinion among wavering Bull Moosers at this stage. Another prominent Bull Mooser who returned to the Republican party in 1915, Medill McCormick of Illinois, hoped to organize a meeting between Roosevelt and Borah where some kind of understanding might be reached that could lead to the nomination of Borah at the 1916 convention.[9]

It seems probable that Borah toyed with the idea of an open bid for the presidential nomination in 1916, but there was one serious drawback to his candidacy which held him back. Idaho, his home state, was one of the least populous states in the Union, and strategically the whole mountain state region was of little value in a presidential election. In normal circumstances a national party would not draw a candidate from such an area unless he were a great national hero or for some reason or other had extraordinary personal strength. Although Borah was looked upon as an attractive candidate for national office, few believed that he had any such tremendous strength, least of all Borah himself. "I do not think it is their intention to go to our part of the country for a candidate," Borah advised a well-wisher in May 1915,[10] and as the convention date neared he grew increasingly firm in the position that he was not a candidate. In November Borah rewrote part of an article about himself for *Collier's Magazine,* which read in part,

Senator Borah realizes that even if the standpat Republicans decide to make any concessions to the progressive element of the party his location will be used against him effectively. He therefore is determined to make no effort to secure the nomination but to give his influence and his ability to the securing of a liberal and advanced platform and the nominaiton of a candidate in harmony with the platform. He knows that Senator Cummins has decided to be a candidate. He speaks highly of Senator Cummins, sympathizes with his candidacy, and will undoubtedly support it

[8] Henry J. Allen to William Allen White, August 19, 1915, White Papers.
[9] McCormick to Borah, Nov. 27, 1915, Borah Papers.
[10] Borah to D. I. Badley, May 30, 1915, *ibid.*

unless the situation convinces him that the progressive forces in the Republican party can make a stronger fight behind some other progressive than his Iowa friend.[11]

So Cummins became the standard bearer for the progressive Republicans in the contest for the presidential nomination.

There were two main features of Albert Cummins's presidential campaign. First, the Iowa Senator attempted to consolidate behind him the progressive wing of the Republican party and to persuade the Old Guard that he was the one candidate capable of winning the support of the Bull Moosers, and hence the election. Second, he attempted to find as much common ground with the conservative wing of the party as was consistent with his stance as a "progressive Republican."

In his attempt to win the approval or at least the tolerance of eastern Republicans, Cummins took moderate and even blatantly conservative stands on a number of the issues. He opposed the establishment of a government-owned nitrate plant at Muscle Shoals, a preparedness measure highly favored by most of the insurgents.[12] He placed great emphasis on the tariff issue. "The tariff," Cummins declared, was "the one, permanent, fundamental, partisan issue," and although there had been some minor differences among Republicans on particular tariff bills from time to time, the Republican party, "taught by experience, tempered by adversity," could frame a good tariff law.[13] In his campaign speeches, Cummins continuously harped on the iniquities of the Underwood tariff of 1913 and charged that it was the loss of revenues caused by this measure that had created the need for the so-called war taxes.[14] Along with Borah and Works, he also found reasons for opposing the appointment of Louis D. Brandeis to the Supreme Court, an act which was praised by La Follette and most independent progressives.

While attempting rather unsuccessfully to establish a measure of rapport with the eastern wing of the party, Cummins

[11] Borah to Mark Sullivan, Nov. 5, 1915, *ibid.*
[12] Sayre, *Cummins,* p. 448.
[13] Manuscript for speech, dated only 1915, Cummins Papers.
[14] New York *Times,* Feb. 13, 1915; *ibid.,* April 6, 1915.

set out to "consolidate the country west of the Mississippi river." [15] To the other insurgents, Cummins denied any "overwhelming ambition" for the presidency, and he told Borah that he would much prefer to see him get the office. But his candidacy was necessary, Cummins said, if "our eastern friends" were not to "walk away with the nomination without serious opposition." The Republicans would lose the election, he argued, if the nomination went to an easterner "whose election would mean to the people generally the restoration of the Old crowd to complete power." [16]

In September 1915, Cummins let it be known that he had given his Iowa supporters "consent to the organization of a campaign on my behalf," [17] and by the end of the year he had apparently made some progress. Congressmen returning to Washington for the new session observed that either Cummins or Theodore Burton of Ohio was the strongest Republican candidate in the western states. Probably Cummins was the stronger of the two, it was thought, but Washington opinion, according to the New York *Times,* was that "the unlikelihood of the eastern Republicans accepting Mr. Cummins as party leader" made Burton an equally strong candidate.[18]

In 1916 Cummins entered his name in a number of primary contests in western states, though he conceded Wisconsin and North Dakota to La Follette, who was a nominal candidate for the presidential nomination once again.[19] In the other progressive Republican states with primary laws, he encountered little opposition. He won all or most of the delegates from Iowa, Minnesota, South Dakota, and Nebraska, but failed to capture the Kansas delegation where the conservatives had controlled the party ever since the progressive bolt in 1912 and 1913. Colorado and Montana also gave their support to Cummins.[20]

---

[15] Cummins to Bristow, June 16, 1915, Bristow Papers.
[16] *Ibid.*; Cummins to Borah, Sept. 3, 1915, Borah Papers.
[17] *Ibid.*
[18] New York *Times,* Nov. 14, 1915.
[19] *Ibid.,* Jan. 27, 1916.
[20] *Ibid.,* March 15, April 22, April 24, May 25, 1916; Des Moines *Register,* June 10, 1916.

But Cummins never really developed much strength outside the north-central states that made up the heartland of Republican insurgency. This area was conceded to be Cummins territory, and he had no serious opposition in the primaries there. When he attempted to move further afield, the results were disastrous. Despite three weeks campaigning in Oregon, a state that had not been unfriendly to progressive Republican candidates in the past, Cummins was buried in the state's presidential primary by Charles Evans Hughes, a candidate who had not campaigned at all and who did not even want his name to be on the ballot.[21] Before the Oregon primary, Cummins had had more committed delegates than any other candidate — 74.[22] He had said that he expected to win "every primary state west of the Mississippi,"[23] and had he been able to do so, he might have been a serious contender at the convention. But the Oregon primary showed that his support was confined to the core of progressive Republican states in the middle west. Cummins did not altogether give up hope of obtaining the nomination after his defeat in Oregon. He had, after all, some 80 delegates pledged to him and he retained a faint hope that the hostility of "the Roosevelt people" to Hughes might give him a chance.[24] But the Oregon disaster really ended whatever chance Cummins might have had for the nomination.

In part the failure of the Cummins presidential campaign in 1916 shows nothing more than the personal weakness of Cummins as a campaigner. He had made an excellent Governor. He was generally admired for his intellectual abilities, possessing, in Senator Clapp's view, "one of the best trained minds I know, with a power of analysis which is absolutely marvelous."[25] He was unsurpassed in the arts of parliamentary debate and maneuver. But he could never match La Follette, Borah, Dolliver, or Beveridge as an orator or stump speaker.

---

[21] New York *Times,* May 21, 1916.
[22] *Ibid.,* May 1, 1916.
[23] *Ibid.,* May 16, 1916.
[24] Cummins to Bristow, May 28, 1916, Bristow Papers.
[25] Clapp to Albert Beveridge, July 1, 1913, Beveridge Papers.

It was a grave misfortune for the insurgents that by 1916 Beveridge had been defeated and had then defected, Dolliver was dead, La Follette had isolated himself from the mainstream of the movement, and Borah's geographical disability made him unavailable. Though he was the equal or superior of these men in many other ways, Cummins could not compete with them as a campaigner.

Yet the very fact that Cummins lacked a great personal appeal as a presidential candidate makes his defeat more meaningful in broad political terms, for without a great campaign style to sustain him, Cummins had to rely on the hard core of progressive Republican sentiment. It seems not unreasonable to suggest that the 100 or so delegates whom La Follette and Cummins brought to the convention of 1916 reflects reasonably accurately the strength of the insurgent movement within the Republican party at the time. It had been all along a minority movement, strong in one or two areas of the country but weak everywhere else. These facts had been obscured by the tumultuous events of the Taft years and especially by the nationwide success of the 1912 Roosevelt boom. The year 1916 brought the hard facts to light.

Even had Cummins shown considerably greater strength in 1916, it seems highly improbable that the Republican Old Guard would ever have consented to his nomination or to that of anyone as far to the left. At times it was suggested that Cummins or Kenyon might be offered the vice-presidential spot on the ticket as a sop to the progressive wing of the party, but few believed seriously that the conservatives would accept a western progressive as the presidential nominee.[26] Everything done and said by the Old Guard leaders since the beginnings of the insurgent revolt in 1909 suggested that they were made of sterner stuff. Defeat was always preferable to victory under a "radical" like Cummins or La Follette.

Furthermore, the whole Cummins strategy of threatening the conservatives with the specter of a Wilson-Bull Moose alliance was completely undermined in 1915 by the rise of for-

---

[26] New York *Times,* May 17, 1916.

eign policy issues and the related question of preparedness. There had never been a complete identity of interest between the Roosevelt men on the one hand and the insurgent Republicans from the west on the other. But if domestic issues had remained in the foreground, the Progressives and the progressive Republicans would probably have been able to re-establish the alliance of 1912 without great difficulty. Instead 1915 saw Roosevelt and the Progressives paying less and less attention to the questions of domestic reform and more and more to the inadequacies of Wilson's preparedness program and the "weakness" and "vacillation" of his dealings with Germany and Mexico. Victor Murdock, national chairman of the Progressive party, declared in September 1915 that preparedness would be the dominant issue in the forthcoming presidential election.[27] There could be little possibility of close cooperation between the two groups under these circumstances, for the insurgents were leaning strongly toward pacificism and nonintervention in face of the threats from abroad. As early as February 1915, Roosevelt was complaining that the insurgent Senators were "the worst crowd we have to deal with," [28] and the feeling was reciprocated. If Roosevelt should run for the presidency "with preparedness as a paramount issue," George Norris stated publicly, "I should oppose him." [29]

In this situation, the Old Guard saw little need to worry about the La Follette-Cummins wing of the party. An altogether different type of candidate could be found to conciliate the Roosevelt forces, and with the Colonel in his 1916 mood, that man would by no means have to be committed to the radical programs of domestic reform that the Progressive party had advocated in 1912. One man seemed to fit the bill above all others. Charles Evans Hughes, Supreme Court Justice and former Governor of New York, had a reputation as a moderate reformer, and he had not been involved in the bitter intra-party strife of 1912. As early as July 1915, Roosevelt had indi-

[27] *Ibid.,* Sept. 23, 1915.
[28] Quoted in Mowry, *Theodore Roosevelt and the Progressive Movement,* p. 321.
[29] New York *Times,* April 7, 1916.

cated that Hughes would be an acceptable compromise candidate. Asked whether the Progressives would amalgamate with
the Republicans in 1916, Roosevelt replied that it all depended
on the presidential nominee. "Suppose the Republicans should
name Justice Hughes for President — I am merely using the
name as a hypothetical case — it would be proper for us to
support him. Our Progressive idea could be embraced in such
a candidate." [30] Roosevelt and his supporters, of course, were
hoping for the nomination not of Hughes but of the Colonel
himself. Still Roosevelt had made it abundantly clear that
Hughes would be acceptable, and in January 1916 when the
Progressive party decided to hold its convention simultane-
ously with the Republicans, thereby holding out the possibility of fusion, George Perkins announced for the Progressives
that a compromise candidate "will not necessarily have to be
Colonel Roosevelt." [31]

Hughes was not exactly a favorite of the Republican Old
Guard. Jacob Gallinger, the Republican minority leader in the
Senate, thought Hughes no more desirable a candidate than
Roosevelt, "neither one of them," he confided to a fellow
standpatter "representing the kind of Republicanism you and
I believe in." [32] But in general the Republican Old Guard
found Hughes a palatable compromise choice, just as Roose-
velt did.[33] "He is the second choice of almost the whole coun-
try," Borah remarked,[34] and on this basis Hughes won the
Republican presidential nomination in 1916.

The insurgents could support Hughes without a serious loss
of face, since he was reckoned to be a progressive of sorts. But
fundamentally the nomination of Hughes represented a compromise between Theodore Roosevelt and the Republican Old
Guard, a deal in which the Republican insurgents played no
important part. Privately they were far from enthusiastic about
the choice of Hughes. "You and I know," Cummins wrote to

[30] *Ibid.,* July 20, 1915.

[31] *Ibid.,* Jan. 12, 1916.

[32] Gallinger to J. O. Lyford, May 23, 1916, Gallinger Papers.

[33] New York *Times,* Dec. 16, 1915.

[34] Borah to E. H. Dewey, March 27, 1916, Borah Papers.

Bristow, "that Hughes has given no evidence of being a progressive." [35] "The trouble with Hughes and Whitman and those New York alleged progressives," Bristow remarked, "is that they think that the progressive movement means that a man should not be an ordinary thief or murderer. They are not sound on the fundamental economic reforms that we are advocating." [36] La Follette made no effort on behalf of Hughes, and the most Norris would say was that Hughes was an acceptable candidate.[37]

But despite their dissatisfaction with Hughes, no prominent progressive Republican deserted him for Wilson during the campaign. "The dominant spirit of this campaign is reunion among republicans," Cummins wrote to his party workers in Iowa. "I take this opportunity to express the hope that in Iowa, republican victory this vital year will be complete and overwhelming." [38] This loyalty is particularly noteworthy in view of the behavior of prominent ex-Bull Moosers and independent progressives in 1916, who flocked to Wilson's support in droves. As Arthur Link has said, to name the progressives who endorsed Wilson in 1916 "is to list virtually the entire leadership of the advanced wing of the progressive movement in the United States." [39] Yet in 1916 the Republican insurgents stuck with Hughes, who as Lodge said, was "in thorough accord with Roosevelt and myself" on international questions,[40] and who was clearly more conservative than Wilson on domestic issues.

By refusing to desert the G.O.P., the insurgents helped Hughes win almost the only victories he scored outside the industrial states. Iowa, Minnesota, Wisconsin, and South Dakota were the only western states except Oregon that gave a ma-

[35] Cummins to Bristow, March 28, 1916, Bristow Papers.

[36] Bristow to Arthur Capper, Feb. 2, 1915, *ibid.* Whitman was Governor of New York.

[37] New York *Times,* June 11, Oct. 26, 1916.

[38] Cummins to Hon. J. A. Johnson, August 10, 1916, Cummins Papers.

[39] Link, *Campaigns for Progressivism and Peace,* p. 124.

[40] Lodge to Sir Otto Trevelyan, July 8, 1916, Lodge Papers.

jority to Hughes in the 1916 election. But although the Republicans did not lose the support of the leading insurgents in the 1916 campaign, they lost the election precisely because they neglected those currents of opinion that the insurgents represented in the party. William Allen White believed that Hughes was defeated in the west because he had no appeal to western progressives and was suspected of being a Wall Street man.[41] The more usual verdict was that Hughes lost in the west because of the peace issue. His association with Roosevelt and other militants and his statement that he would have broken off diplomatic relations with Germany over the *Lusitania* incident were held to have been the crucial factors.[42] Whatever the case, it can be said that the Republican party lost the election because it neglected the opinions of its progressive wing, which stood for both peace abroad and reform at home. Hughes, Bristow complained after the convention, seemed to think that he could satisfy the progressives by including Roosevelt's ideas in the platform, which showed that "he is very much mistaken . . . as to what the progressive policies are." [43] The conservatives had passed over the midwestern insurgents and made their deal with Roosevelt, hoping thereby to win back the bolters of 1912 with minimal concessions to progressive doctrines. But in doing so they made a bad tactical error, for in 1916 Theodore Roosevelt was no longer in tune with the sentiments of the west. In one sense then, the insurgents were victorious in defeat.

On the other hand the Old Guard won the more lasting victory. In 1912 Taft, Root, and the other leaders of the Old Guard had reasoned that it was better to keep control of the party while losing the election than to win the election while surrendering the party to Rooseveltian radicalism. At that time they had assumed that Democratic rule would be short-lived and that the Republicans would probably return to power in 1916. In this they were mistaken, but in the long run the un-

---

[41] William Allen White to Theodore Roosevelt, Nov. 28, 1916, and Dec. 27, 1916, White Papers.

[42] Link, *Campaigns for Progressivism and Peace,* p. 162.

[43] Bristow to Howard J. Clark, June 26, 1914, Bristow Papers.

bending attitude that the Republican conservatives had maintained in the face of the insurgent revolt paid off. Eventually a conservative reaction against Wilsonian progressivism did set in to bring the Republicans back to power, and when that moment came, the party was still under the control of safe, conservative hands. The Old Guard had good reason to congratulate itself that in 1912 and 1916 it had kept the taint of western progressivism well away from the centers of party power, for in the balmy days of the 1920's the Old Guard no longer had to choose between conservatism and victory. It could have both.

The insurgent leaders were neither stupid men nor inept politicians. Indeed, as parliamentarians, orators, and executives at the state level, they had few peers in the progressive era. In their home states most of them maintained their power throughout the Taft and Wilson years, and from 1909 to 1912 they capitalized on their pivotal position in Congress with great shrewdness. The insurgents' goals, however, were not limited to staying in office and exerting an influence on legislation when their party was in power. They continuously made it plain that they were seeking national power, a task for which insurgent tactics were simply inadequate.

At the root of their problem was the one-party background in which they had been nurtured. Committed to the Republican party, they were unable or unwilling to risk an alliance with the Democrats or to experiment with a third party. Yet inside the G.O.P. they were too small a minority to be able to challenge the conservative leadership effectively. The most they could do was to threaten the Old Guard that if it failed to respond to insurgent demands the party would be defeated, an argument to which the conservatives remained impervious.

In part the insurgents were victims of the federal system. A political style which worked admirably in states like Kansas and Wisconsin failed in Washington, D.C. They were also victims of a party system and a partisan sentiment that had been shaped by issues and events no longer relevant to their own times. Even at the height of the insurgent revolt when the prestige of the Old Guard was at an all-time low, the progressive Republican leaders from the north-central states judged that their constituents would not support a complete break with the Republican party. Nor did the insurgent leaders themselves show any great inclination to make that break themselves. In the long run Republicanism proved to be a more enduring force than progressivism.

# chapter twelve

# Epilogue

The year 1917 marked a decisive turning point for the Republican insurgents. Prior to that date their major problem had been how to reconcile their isolationist-progressive views with their Republicanism; afterwards it was how to justify an ideology that was not merely out of place in the Republican party but that collided headlong with the dominant political trends in the nation at large.

American entry into the European war threatened briefly to wipe out the insurgent movement altogether. Though pacifist-isolationist opposition to intervention crumbled rapidly after the Germans began their campaign of unrestricted submarine warfare in February 1917, the insurgent leaders in Congress were among the last to give up the struggle for peace. In March, a dozen Senators including Clapp, Cummins, Gronna, Kenyon, La Follette, Norris, and Works filibustered to death an administration bill that would have given the President power to arm American ships against submarine attack. For this action they were condemned by President Wilson as "a little group of willful men," and vilified by the national press as traitors and pro-Germans. When the war resolution itself came before Congress, La Follette, Norris, and Gronna were among the six Senators who dared to vote against it.

Having played a prominent role in the fight against intervention, the insurgents were highly vulnerable to political reprisals in the climate of hysterical superpatriotism that the war engendered. Nevertheless Republican insurgency survived the

World War. Though Wilson had charged that the "willful men" represented no opinion but their own, the truth was that pacifist sentiment was strong in many rural areas of the south and west and particularly strong in the north-central states with their large German-American populations. Moreover enthusiasm for the war soon began to wane, and as it did the public stature of La Follette and others who had opposed intervention could only increase.

The struggle over ratification of the Versailles treaty greatly aided the rehabilitation of the Republican insurgents in national politics. Nearly all the leading insurgent Senators were "irreconcilables" or "strong reservationists," and on this issue they were joined in opposition to Wilson by the Republican conservatives. In a manner reminiscent of the Republican left-right coalition against Wilson's "New Freedom," the anti-imperialist isolationism of La Follette joined hands with the militant nationalism of Lodge in opposition to Wilson's treaty. While their fight against intervention in the war had isolated and nearly destroyed the Republican insurgents, their stand against the League won them a place in a powerful and ultimately victorious coalition.

On domestic issues, however, there could be little harmony between insurgent and regular Republicans in the postwar decade. The conservatives had demonstrated little inclination to compromise with the progressive wing of the party in the prewar years. Why should they be more conciliatory now when the Republican party swept to landslide victories at the polls with unabashedly conservative candidates? Some of the old insurgents, most notably Albert Cummins, reacted to this unfavorable situation by moving steadily toward more conservative positions, even to the point of becoming closely identified with the Harding and Coolidge administrations.

Yet Republican insurgency remained very much alive in the 1920's. Though some of the old progressive leaders became more conservative or left the political scene, the insurgent ranks were swelled by such new faces as Senators Smith Brookhart of Iowa, Peter Norbeck of South Dakota, Lynn Frazier and Edwin Ladd of North Dakota, and R. W. Howell of Nebraska. There is little mystery about the origins of this new phase of agrarian radicalism in the Republican middle west. Despite the general prosperity of the period, the 1920's were years of chronic agricultural depression, and in these years the Republican progressives in Congress were primarily concerned with the farm problem. They favored measures to extend credit facilities to farmers and their customers; to regulate meat packers, stockyards, and grain exchanges; to provide tariff protection for agricultural products; to promote cooperative marketing; to raise farm prices directly through the McNary-Haugen system; and so on.

This concentration upon the special problem of agriculture had not been typical of the insurgent movement in the Taft and Wilson years. Although the earlier insurgents were closely oriented to the values and problems of rural America, they had fought their great battles over broad national questions such as the control of the trusts and the maintenance of peace. Though never close to the centers of power, they had been deeply concerned with all the central political issues of their day. An altogether more provincial quality was apparent in the insurgency of the 1920's, representing as it did the disaffection of a minority in an era of general conservatism.

On the other hand the most prominent progressive Republican leaders of the 1920's were the same men who led the insurgent movement in the Taft and Wilson years, and the newcomers such as Brookhart and Frazier represented the same north-central states that had spawned the earlier insurgency. Moreover, though the younger insurgents were primarily concerned with the new and difficult problem of depressed farm prices, they tended to draw heavily on the old progressive ideology with its emphasis on popular government and the evils of corporate power. It may be doubted whether the destruction of the trusts or any of the other progressive remedies would have done much to help American agriculture in the 1920's, but the antimonopoly rhetoric favored by La Follette and the other insurgents served as a rallying point for agrarian discontent.

In the 1920's most of the political stratagems tried out by

the insurgents in the prewar years were revived. Of these, bipartisan alignment with the Democrats was still the most effective. Progressive Republicans led by Senator Kenyon of Iowa played a prominent role in the formation of the farm bloc in which Democrats and Republicans from farm states combined to promote agricultural legislation, and they joined the Democrats in opposing such standpat measures as the Smoot-Hawley tariff of 1930. The insurgents also attempted once again to organize their forces within the Republican ranks to put pressure upon the party leadership. In 1923, for instance, 50 Republican Congressmen formed a "Progressive Republican Congress" in an effort to capitalize on the gains the insurgents had made in the midterm elections. The year before Senator Borah had predicted that if the Republican party did not change its economic policies a third party would sweep the country, a warning similar to many issued by the insurgents during the Bull Moose days. Finally the 1920's saw another attempt at a third party, La Follette's Progressive party of 1924. Only the more radical insurgents were drawn into this ill-fated movement.

With the Great Depression of the 1930's, Republican insurgency moved in a new direction. Totally disgusted with the Hoover administration by 1932, a number of prominent progressive Republicans bolted their party and endorsed the Democratic party's nominee for President, Franklin D. Roosevelt. They included Senators Robert La Follette Jr., George Norris, Hiram Johnson, Smith Brookhart, and Bronson Cutting. Unlike Wilson before him, Roosevelt cultivated progressive Republican support in every conceivable way. He appointed prominent progressive Republicans like Harold Ickes and Henry Wallace to high posts in his administration and offered appointments to Bronson Cutting, Philip La Follette and others. He rewarded the insurgent Senators who supported his programs in Congress with federal patronage and backed them when they came up for re-election. He initiated a legislative program that won the general approval of the leading insurgents and some parts of which were closely tailored to their special interests. One of the very first products of the

New Deal, for instance, was the Tennessee Valley Authority, a direct outgrowth of the insurgents' long battle for public power.

The insurgents in Congress did not give unquestioning approval to every New Deal measure. Many of them were suspicious of the NRA, and most opposed the administration's reciprocal tariff policies. Nor did any prominent insurgent Republican officially join the Democratic party. Yet it seems fair to say that by 1936 the New Deal had absorbed the Republican insurgent movement where it still existed. In that year several insurgent Senators again endorsed Roosevelt's candidacy, and most of the others remained silent during the campaign rather than oppose him.

In the late 1930's and early 1940's the isolationist views of some insurgents brought them into conflict with the administration on matters of foreign policy. But by now it was becoming scarcely possible to speak of an insurgent movement any more. Republican progressivism was rapidly losing its grip on the north-central states where it had been entrenched for so long. In Iowa and the prairie states — Kansas, Nebraska, and the Dakotas — a reaction against the urban-oriented New Deal developed during these years. Instead of pro-New Deal insurgents like Norris and Norbeck, these states began sending to Congress conservative Republicans who denounced the power of the federal government in much the same terms as the insurgents had once denounced the power of the trusts. The new liberalism fared better in Minnesota and Wisconsin with their larger urban populations, but it found its voice in new forms of organization. In 1934 the younger La Follettes led their supporters out of the Republican party and formed a Progressive party in Wisconsin. This organization dissolved in the 1940's, and Robert La Follette Jr. ran for re-election to the Senate in 1946 as a Republican; but it was the Democratic party that emerged eventually as the party of liberalism in Wisconsin. In Minnesota the process was more explicit. The Farmer-Labor party of Minnesota, founded after World War I, dominated the government of the state in the 1930's and formally amalgamated with the Democrats in the 1940's.

The rise of Harold Stassen and the "young Republicans" in Minnesota during the late 1930's might be seen as a continuation of the progressive tradition in the Republican party, but in reality Stassen, Dewey, and younger Republican liberals of the 1930's and 1940's had little in common with the insurgents of the Taft and Wilson years. The new Republican liberals drew their support not from the farms and small towns of the prairies, but from the larger urbanized states of the east. They were noted for their willingness to accommodate the changes in government and society wrought by the New Deal, but they did not offer more radical programs of their own, as the insurgents had done. They emphasized neither the extension of "popular government" nor anti-trust programs.

The Republican insurgents were never close to national power after 1912, but their movement lingered on as long as agrarian radicalism remained alive. When the demand for innovation in government moved from the country to the city, Republican insurgency disappeared from the American scene.

# Bibliography     Index

# Bibliography

Primary Sources

*1. Manuscript Collections*

NELSON W. ALDRICH PAPERS, Library of Congress, Washington, D.C.

ALBERT J. BEVERIDGE PAPERS, Library of Congress, Washington, D.C.

WILLIAM E. BORAH PAPERS, Library of Congress, Washington, D.C.

JOSEPH L. BRISTOW PAPERS, Kansas State Historical Society, Topeka, Kansas.

MOSES E. CLAPP PAPERS, Minnesota Historical Society, St. Paul, Minnesota.

COE L. CRAWFORD PAPERS, South Dakota State Historical Society, Pierre, South Dakota.

ALBERT B. CUMMINS PAPERS, Iowa State Department of History and Archives, Des Moines, Iowa.

JONATHAN P. DOLLIVER PAPERS, State Historical Society of Iowa, Iowa City, Iowa.

JOHN J. ESCH PAPERS, State Historical Society of Wisconsin, Madison, Wisconsin.

JACOB H. GALLINGER PAPERS, New Hampshire Historical Society, Concord, New Hampshire.

HERBERT S. HADLEY PAPERS, Western Historical Manuscripts Collection, University of Missouri, Columbia, Missouri.

NILS P. HAUGEN PAPERS, State Historical Society of Wisconsin, Madison, Wisconsin.

JOHN A. T. HULL PAPERS, Iowa State Department of History and Archives, Des Moines, Iowa.

JOHN C. LACEY PAPERS, Iowa State Department of History and Archives, Des Moines, Iowa.

HENRY CABOT LODGE PAPERS, Massachusetts Historical Society, Boston, Massachusetts.

JAMES MANAHAN PAPERS, Minnesota Historical Society, St. Paul, Minnesota.

JAMES R. MANN PAPERS, Library of Congress, Washington, D.C.

KNUTE NELSON PAPERS, Minnesota Historical Society, St. Paul, Minnesota.

GEORGE W. NORRIS PAPERS, Library of Congress, Washington, D.C.

GEORGE D. PERKINS PAPERS, Iowa State Department of History and Archives, Des Moines, Iowa.

GIFFORD PINCHOT PAPERS, Library of Congress, Washington, D.C.

MILES POINDEXTER PAPERS, University of Virginia Library, Charlottesville, Virginia.

THEODORE ROOSEVELT PAPERS, Library of Congress, Washington, D.C.

ELIHU ROOT PAPERS, Library of Congress, Washington, D.C.

JAMES A. TAWNEY PAPERS, Minnesota Historical Society, St. Paul, Minnesota.

WILLIAM HOWARD TAFT PAPERS, Library of Congress, Washington, D.C.

WILLIAM ALLEN WHITE PAPERS, Library of Congress, Washington, D.C.

JOHN D. WORKS PAPERS, University of California Library, Berkeley, California.

## 2. Government Documents

*Biographical Directory of the American Congress, 1774–1949,* House Document 607, 81 Congress, 2 Session.

*Congressional Record,* 61–64 Congresses, 1909–1917.

*Congressional Directory,* 1909–1916.

*Senate Documents,* 61 Congress, 2 Series, Vol. 58.

## 3. Newspapers

Des Moines *Register,* 1912–1916.

Helena *Independent,* 1912.

Kansas City *Star,* 1912–1914.
Minneapolis *Journal,* 1912, 1913, 1916.
New York *Times,* 1909–1916.
New York *Tribune,* 1909–1916.

*4. Contemporary Periodicals*

*Harper's Weekly Magazine,* 1909–1916.
*La Follette's Weekly* (*La Follette's Magazine* after 1915), 1909–
     1916.
*Literary Digest,* 1912–1916.
*New Republic,* 1915–1916.
*Saturday Evening Post,* 1912–1916.

*5. Contemporary Books and Published Correspondence*

*Chicago Daily News Almanac and Yearbook,* 1889–1913.
DeWitt, Benjamin P., *The Progressive Movement.* New York:
     Macmillan, 1915.
Dreier, Thomas, *Heroes of Insurgency.* Boston: Human Life
     Publishing, 1910.
Gardner, Constance, ed., *Some Letters of Augustus Peabody
     Gardner.* Boston: Houghton Mifflin, 1920.
Haines, Lynn, *Law Making in America: the Story of the 1911–
     1912 Session of the Sixty-Second Congress.* Bethesda, Mary-
     land: Haines, 1912.
———, *The Senate from 1907 to 1912.* Washington, D.C.: Na-
     tional Capital, 1912.
La Follette, Robert, *Autobiography.* Madison: University of
     Wisconsin Press, 1911, 1960.
Morison, Elting, ed., *The Letters of Theodore Roosevelt.* 8
     vols. Cambridge, Mass.: Harvard University Press, 1951–
     1956.
*New York Tribune Almanac,* 1913–1917.
Roosevelt, Theodore, *The New Nationalism.* ed. William E.
     Leuchtenburg. Englewood Cliffs, N.J.: Prentice-Hall, 1961.

*6. Interviews*

An interview with Alfred M. Landon, May 8, 1963, Topeka,
     Kansas.

Secondary Sources

*1. Books and Articles*

Abrams, Richard M., *Conservatism in a Progressive Era: Massachusetts Politics, 1900–1912.* Cambridge, Mass.: Harvard University Press, 1964.

Allen, Howard W., "Miles Poindexter and the Progressive Movement," *Pacific Northwest Quarterly*, LIII, No. 3 (July 1962) 114.

Atkinson, Charles R., *The Committee on Rules and the Overthrow of Speaker Cannon.* New York: Columbia University Press, 1911.

Blegan, Theodore C., *Minnesota: a History of the State.* Minneapolis: University of Minnesota Press, 1963.

Blum, John M., *The Republican Roosevelt.* Cambridge, Mass.: Harvard University Press, 1954.

———, *Woodrow Wilson and the Politics of Morality.* Boston: Little Brown, 1956.

Bolles, Blair, *Tyrant from Illinois: Uncle Joe Cannon's Experiment with Personal Power.* New York: Norton, 1951.

Bowden, Robert D., *Boies Penrose: Symbol of an Era.* New York: Greenberg, 1937.

Bowers, Claude G., *Beveridge and the Progressive Era.* Boston: Houghton Mifflin, 1932.

Braeman, John, "Seven Progressives," *Business History Review*, XXXV (Winter 1961), 581.

Bryn-Jones, David, *Frank B. Kellogg: a Biography.* New York: G. P. Putnam's Sons, 1937.

Butler, Nicholas Murray, *Across the Busy Years.* 2 vols. New York: C. Scribner's Sons, 1939–1940.

Curti, Merle, *Peace or War: the American Struggle, 1636–1936.* New York: W. W. Norton, 1936.

Davenport, Walter, *Power and Glory: the Life of Boies Penrose.* New York: G. P. Putnam's Sons, 1931.

Davis, Oscar King, *Released for Publication: Some Inside Political History of Theodore Roosevelt and His Times, 1898–1918.* Boston: Houghton Mifflin, 1925.

Fausold, Martin L., *Gifford Pinchot: Bull Moose Progressive.* Syracuse, N.Y.: Syracuse University Press, 1961.

Fite, Gilbert C., *Peter Norbeck: Prairie Statesman.* Columbia: University of Missouri Press, 1948.

Garraty, John A., *Henry Cabot Lodge: A Biography*. New York: Knopf, 1953.

———, *Right Hand Man: the Life of George W. Perkins*. New York: Harper, 1960.

Gwinn, William Rea, *Uncle Joe Cannon, Archfoe of Insurgency: A History of the Rise and Fall of Cannonism*. New York: Bookman Associates, 1957.

Hapgood, Norman, *The Changing Years: Reminiscences*. New York: Farrar and Rinehart, 1930.

Harbaugh, William Henry, *Power and Responsibility: the Life and Times of Theodore Roosevelt*. New York: Farrar, Strauss, and Cudahy, 1961.

Haugen, Nils P., "Pioneer and Political Reminiscences," *Wisconsin. Magazine of History*, XII, No. 3 (March 1929), 280.

Hechler, Kenneth W., *Insurgency: Personalities and Politics of the Taft Era*. New York: Columbia University Press, 1940.

Ickes, Harold, "Who Killed the Progressive Party," *American Historical Review*, XLVI (1941), 306.

Jessup, Philip C., *Elihu Root*. 2 vols. New York: Dodd Mead, 1938.

Johnson, Claudius O., *Borah of Idaho*. New York: Longmans Green, 1936.

Johnson, Walter, *William Allen White's America*. New York: Holt, 1947.

Josephson, Matthew, *The President-Makers, 1896–1919*. New York: Harcourt Brace, 1940.

La Follette, Belle C. and Fola, *Robert M. La Follette*. 2 vols. New York: Macmillan, 1953.

Leopold, Richard W., *Elihu Root and the Conservative Tradition*. Boston: Little Brown, 1954.

Levine, Daniel, *Varieties of Reform Thought*. Madison: State Historical Society of Wisconsin, 1964.

Lief, Alfred, *Democracy's Norris: the Biography of a Lonely Crusade*. New York: Stackpole Sons, 1939.

Link, Arthur S., *Wilson*. (vol. 1, *The Road to the White House;* vol. 2, *The New Freedom;* vol. 3, *The Struggle for Neutrality;* vol. 4. *Confusions and Crises;* vol. 5, *Campaigns for Progressivism and Peace*.) Princeton, N.J.: Princeton University Press, 1947–1965.

———, *Woodrow Wilson and the Progressive Era, 1910–1917*. New York: Harper, 1954.

Lowitt, Richard, *George W. Norris: the Making of a Progressive, 1861–1912*. Syracuse, N.Y.: Syracuse University Press, 1963.

McGeary, M. Nelson, *Gifford Pinchot: Forester-Politician*. Princeton, N.J.: Princeton University Press, 1960.

McKenna, Marion C., *Borah*. Ann Arbor: University of Michigan Press, 1961.

Mason, Alpheus Thomas, *Brandeis: a Free Man's Life*. New York: Viking, 1946.

Maxwell, Robert S., *La Follette and the Rise of the Progressives in Wisconsin*. Madison: State Historical Society of Wisconsin, 1956.

May, Earnest R., *The World War and American Isolation, 1914–1917*. Cambridge, Mass.: Harvard University Press, 1959.

Moos, Malcolm, *The Republicans: a History of Their Party*. New York: Random House, 1956.

Morison, Elting, *Turmoil and Tradition: a Study of the Life and Times of Henry L. Stimson*. Boston: Houghton Mifflin, 1960.

Mowry, George E., *The California Progressives*. Berkeley: University of California Press, 1951.

———, *The Era of Theodore Roosevelt and the Birth of Modern America, 1900–1912*. New York: Harper, 1958.

———, *Theodore Roosevelt and the Progressive Movement*. Madison: University of Wisconsin Press, 1946.

Neuberger, Richard L., and S. B. Kahn, *Integrity: the Life of George Norris*. New York: Vanguard, 1937.

Norris, George W., *Fighting Liberal: the Autobiography of George W. Norris*. New York: Macmillan, 1945.

———, "Why I Believe in the Direct Primary," *Annals of the American Academy of Political and Social Science*, CVI (March 1923), 23.

Nye, Russel B., *Midwestern Progressive Politics: a Historical Study of its Origins and Development, 1870–1950*. East Lansing: Michigan State University Press, 1951.

Perkins, Dexter, *Charles Evans Hughes and American Democratic Statesmanship*. Boston: Little Brown, 1956.

Pinchot, Amos, *History of the Progressive Party, 1912–1916*, ed. Helene M. Hooker. New York: New York University Press, 1958.

Pringle, Henry F., *The Life and Times of William Howard Taft: a Biography*. 2 vols. New York: Farrar and Rinehart, 1939.

———, *Theodore Roosevelt: A Biography*. New York: Harcourt Brace, 1931.

Pusey, Merlo J., *Charles Evans Hughes*. 2 vols. New York: Macmillan, 1951.

Rosewater, Victor, *Backstage in 1912: the Inside Story of the Split Republican Convention*. Philadelphia: Dorrance, 1932.

Ross, Thomas Richard, *Jonathan Prentiss Dolliver: a study in Political Integrity and Independence*. Iowa City: State Historical Society of Iowa, 1958.

Sageser, A. Bower, "Joseph L. Bristow: the Editor's Road to Politics," *Kansas Historical Quarterly* (Summer 1964), p. 153.

Socolofsky, Homer E., *Arthur Capper: Publisher, Politician, and Philanthropist*. Lawrence: University of Kansas Press, 1962.

Stephenson, Nathaniel W., *Nelson W. Aldrich: a Leader in American Politics*. New York: C. Scribner's Sons, 1930.

Walters, Everett, *Joseph Benson Foraker: an Uncompromising Republican*. Columbus: Ohio History Press, 1948.

Warner, Hoyt L., *Progressivism in Ohio, 1897–1917*. Columbus: Ohio State University Press, 1964.

Watson, James E., *As I Knew Them: Memoirs of James E. Watson*. Indianapolis: Bobbs-Merrill, 1936.

White, William Allen, *Autobiography*. New York: Macmillan, 1946.

Wilensky, Norman M., *Conservatives in the Progressive Era: The Taft Republicans of 1912*. Gainesville: University of Florida Press, 1965.


## 2. Unpublished doctoral dissertations

Allen, Howard W., *Miles Poindexter: a Political Biography*. University of Washington, 1959.

Armin, Calvin Perry, *Coe L. Crawford and the Progressive Movement in South Dakota*. University of Colorado, 1957.

Forth, William Stuart, *Wesley L. Jones: a Political Biography*. University of Washington, 1962.

Phillips, William Weiland, *The Life of Asle J. Gronna: a*

*Self-made Man of the Prairies.* University of Missouri, 1958.
Pike, Albert Heisey Jr., *Jonathan Bourne Jr.: Progressive.* University of Oregon, 1957.
Sayre, Ralph Mills, *Albert Baird Cummins and the Progressive Movement in Iowa.* Columbia, 1958.

# Index

# Harvard Historical Monographs

*\* Out of Print*

1. Athenian Tribal Cycles in the Hellenistic Age. By W. S. Ferguson. 1932.
2. The Private Record of an Indian Governor-Generalship: The Correspondence of Sir John Shore, Governor-General, with Henry Dundas, President of the Board of Control, 1793–1798. Edited by Holden Furber. 1933.
3. The Federal Railway Land Subsidy Policy of Canada. By J. B. Hedges. 1934.
4. Russian Diplomacy and the Opening of the Eastern Question in 1838 and 1839. By P. E. Mosley. 1934.*
5. The First Social Experiments in America: A Study in the Development of Spanish Indian Policy in the Sixteenth Century. By Lewis Hanke. 1935.*
6. British Propaganda at Home and in the United States from 1914 to 1917. By J. D. Squires. 1935.
7. Bernadotte and the Fall of Napoleon. By F. D. Scott. 1935.*
8. The Incidence of the Terror during the French Revolution: A Statistical Interpretation. By Donald Greer. 1935.*
9. French Revolutionary Legislation on Illegitimacy, 1789–1804. By Crane Brinton. 1936.
10. An Ecclesiastical Barony of the Middle Ages: The Bishopric of Bayeux, 1066–1204. By S. E. Gleason. 1936.
11. Chinese Traditional Historiography. By C. S. Gardner. 1938. Rev. ed., 1961.
12. Studies in Early French Taxation. By J. R. Strayer and C. H. Taylor. 1939.
13. Muster and Review: A Problem of English Military Administration, 1420–1440. By R. A. Newhall. 1940.*

14. Portuguese Voyages to America in the Fifteenth Century. By S. E. Morison. 1940.\*
15. Argument from Roman Law in Political Thought, 1200–1600. By M. P. Gilmore, 1941.\*
16. The Huancavelica Mercury Mine: A Contribution to the History of the Bourbon Renaissance in the Spanish Empire. By A. P. Whitaker. 1941.\*
17. The Palace School of Muhammad the Conqueror. By Barnette Miller. 1941.
18. A Cistercian Nunnery in Mediaeval Italy: The Story of Rifreddo in Saluzzo, 1220–1300. By Catherine E. Boyd. 1943.\*
19. Vassi and Fideles in the Carolingian Empire. By C. E. Odegaard. 1945.\*
20. Judgment by Peers. By Barnaby C. Keeney. 1949.
21. The Election to the Russian Constituent Assembly of 1917. By O. H. Radkey. 1950.
22. Conversion and the Poll Tax in Early Islam. By Daniel C. Dennett. 1950.\*
23. Albert Gallatin and the Oregon Problem. By Frederick Merk. 1950.\*
24. The Incidence of the Emigration during the French Revolution. By Donald Greer. 1951.\*
25. Alterations of the Words of Jesus as Quoted in the Literature of the Second Century. By Leon E. Wright, 1952.\*
26. Liang Ch'i Ch'ao and the Mind of Modern China. By Joseph R. Levenson. 1953.
27. The Japanese and Sun Yat-sen. By Marius B. Jansen. 1954.
28. English Politics in the Early Eighteenth Century. By Robert Walcott, Jr. 1956.
29. The Founding of the French Socialist Party (1893–1905). By Aaron Noland. 1956.
30. British Labour and the Russian Revolution, 1917–1924. By Stephen Richards Graubard. 1956.\*
31. RKFDV: German Resettlement and Population Policy, 1939–1945. By Robert L. Koehl. 1957.
32. Disarmament and Peace in British Politics, 1914–1919. By Gerda Richards Crosby. 1957.
33. Concordia Mundi: The Career and Thought of Guillaume Postel (1510–1581). By W. J. Bouwsma. 1957.
34. Bureaucracy, Aristocracy, and Autocracy: The Prussian Experience, 1660–1815. By Hans Rosenberg. 1958.